S0-BEZ-413

THE STORY OF TUNNELS

Roy Chadwick & Martin C Knights

ANDRE DEUTSCH

CONTENTS

For Francis, Hazel,
Jane and Thomas

Our aim in writing this book has
been to bring the past and present
of tunnelling alive.
We thank the international tunnelling organisations for providing
information and illustrations, and
in particular David Martin, editor
of 'Tunnels and Tunnelling'.

First published in 1988 by
André Deutsch Limited
105–106 Great Russell Street,
London WC1B 3LJ

Copyright © 1988 by
Roy Chadwick and Martin C Knights

All rights reserved

*British Library Cataloguing
in Publication Data*

Chadwick, Roy
  The story of tunnels.
  1. Tunneling – Juvenile literature
  I. Title   II. Knights, Martin
  624.1'93   TA807
  ISBN 0 233 98170 5

Photoset by
David John Services Ltd.,
Farnham Royal, Berks.

Printed in Hong Kong

INTRODUCTION   3

1 **HOW TUNNELLERS SOLVE PROBLEMS**   The nature
of the ground and the basics of tunnelling.   5

2 **THE FIRST TUNNELS**   Primitive tunnellers and the
Ancient Greeks and Romans.   9

3 **TREASURES OF THE EARTH**   Mining, its economic and
social history. The techniques of tunnellers in underground
mines.   12

4 **UNDERPINNING CIVILISATION**   Water through
tunnels for irrigation, drinking, sewerage and hydro-
electricity. Tunnels for power supply, war and science.   21
PHOTOFEATURE
Mountain caverns for hydro-electric power.   29

5 **THE STORY OF CAVERNS**   Caverns to store fuel, food
and nuclear waste. Underground hospitals, communities,
workplaces and sports centres.   35

6 **TUNNELS FOR TRANSPORT**   200 years of transport
tunnels, for canals, roads, railways, metro systems and even air
travel.   38

7 **MOVING MOUNTAINS**   Historic tunnels which have
pierced great mountains, and the tunnelling techniques
developed within them.   46

8 **TUNNELLING UNDERWATER**   Crossing under
powerful rivers and important seaways, and the techniques of
working in wet ground.   54
PHOTOFEATURE
Tunnellers at work under the River Mersey on the first and
second road tunnels.   60

9 **THE CHANNEL TUNNEL**   The saga from 1802 to 1993
with details of the rail service now being built and
consequences.   67

10 **TUNNELS OF THE FUTURE**   Will tunnels float in the
sea? Will we be able to travel to any city in the world in 42.2
minutes? Will we tunnel under the sea from land for oil?   75

11 **TUNNEL BUILDERS OF TODAY AND TOMORROW**
The skills, knowledge and education of the people who build
tunnels. How you could become a tunneller.   77
PHOTOFEATURE
Tunnelling machines and techniques of today.   83

INDEX   94

INTRODUCTION

Fig. 1 *This is the largest machine ever built for boring through hard rock. It was first used in Chicago in 1980, and then sold to China for use on a hydro-electric project. (The Robbins Co, USA)*

People who lived in caves long ago scratched into the rock and dug the first tunnels.

Today a tunneller may sit at a computer terminal and program a remote controlled boring machine deep underground to do all the digging.

Yet, even now, every big tunnel is a journey into the unknown, because however much testing we do, we can never know for sure what will happen underground.

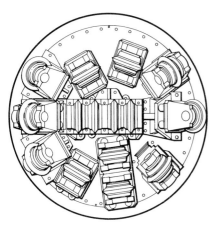

Fig. 2 *Layout of the teeth of a TBM (Tunnel Boring Machine) (T&T)*

Big tunnels still challenge the power of nature, and take tunnellers many miles from home for years at a time to work in primitive conditions. On their way to the work face, tunnellers may be hurled in a bucket at 50km an hour down a deep shaft in total darkness, their weight supported only by a 5cm cable.

The way we live today owes a lot to tunnels which have been used to mine the earth's resources; to bring power and fresh water to cities; for sewage and drainage; to create hydro-electric and nuclear power; to transport people by canal, road and railway, under cities and rivers and through great mountain ranges.

The story of tunnels is one of giant projects, of unbelievable hardship and sacrifice, or immense personal and team achievement. It is also the story of how technical developments have helped to overcome the restrictions of nature.

This book tells these stories and shows how you could become a tunneller of the future.

Fig. 4 *The teeth of a TBM. (Spie Batignolles, France)*

Fig. 3 *Cutter paths on the rock face. (T&T)*

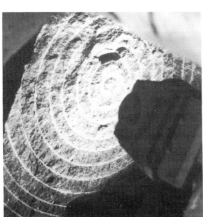

4

Fig. 5 *This steel mould will be placed in a section of newly bored tunnel. Concrete will be poured behind it where it will make a strong wall, then the mould will be moved along to the next section. (Spie Batignolles, France)*

Fig. 6 *Shotcrete, a liquid concrete, being sprayed onto a tunnel wall to reinforce it. (Putzmeister, Germany)*

1
HOW TUNNELLERS SOLVE PROBLEMS

Tunnellers throughout the ages have faced the same basic problems and in talking to each other about them have developed a vocabulary of their own.

The roof of a bored tunnel is called the crown. The tunnel shape is usually circular or arched. A tunnel is always horizontal or sloping. If the hole is vertical it is called a shaft. The entrance to a tunnel is called a portal. If a tunnel is widened for storage or as workspace it is called a cavern.

Most tunnels are long holes in the ground which lead from one place to another; to be used safely they need firm bases and solid walls and arches.

When a tunnel is dug, the sand or clay or soil or rock which has to be taken

THE NATURE OF THE GROUND

The ground beneath us is not as solid as we think when we walk on it. The Earth's crust rests on constantly moving plates which have moved violently enough in the past to thrust up great mountains of solid rock such as the Alps and Rockies. On top of the uneven layers of solid rock and nestling in the crevices between them is soft ground which has been created by rock erosion caused by wind, water and chemicals. Mixed into the eroded rock are the remains of plant and animal life and the rubble of previous human activity. Over centuries soft ground is compressed by weight above. This is usually gradual, but during the Ice Ages much compression took place under the weight of glaciers. Soft ground is deeper in valleys where plant life and habitation have been more dense.

GRAVITY, PRESSURE AND STRESS

Gravity is the force which draws all things towards a dense mass. The Earth has a gravitational pull which not only makes it difficult for us to leave its surface, but means that the more things are piled on top of each other the harder they press on what is underneath.

However, as Newton confirmed, every action provokes an opposite reaction and the Earth pushes back against the pressure from above.

When tunnellers make a hole in the ground, pressure in the ground pushes in on it. In order to keep a hole to the shape they want, tunnellers must strengthen and support it.

away is called spoil – and there can be a lot of it. Excavation of the Channel Tunnel linking Britain and France will produce 9,000,000 cubic metres of spoil.

Tunnellers often have to contend with great pressures from above, of water when digging under rivers, of immense weight when excavating through mountains.

In cities they may be only a few metres below the surface and have to be very careful not to disturb the foundations of buildings or other tunnels and pipes.

TUNNEL ROUTES

The route of a tunnel depends on its use and location. For mining, shafts are sunk to the seam, and tunnels are either horizontal or follow the contour of the seam; while transport tunnellers have to consider the gradients up which traffic can travel, and a tunnel carrying water or oil is likely to slope.

If a tunnel is near the surface it may be easier and cheaper to dig a trench, build the tunnel and cover it. This method, known as cut and cover, is sometimes used for underwater tunnels, when, instead of digging under the lake, river or sea, sections of prefabricated tunnel are lowered into a trench, then joined and covered over.

Geologists and surveyors help tunnellers to find the cheapest safe routes. They use their knowledge of gravity, and trigonometry, and assess the water content, heat, chemical composition, solidity and gas content of the ground which has to be tunnelled through.

Because no one can be sure about ground conditions a small pilot tunnel is sometimes dug ahead of the main tunnel to test the ground. The side panels of this book will help you understand some of the problems.

Fig. 7 *A mould in which concrete is pre-cast before being fitted to line a tunnel. (Charcon Tunnels UK)*

Fig. 8   *A pumping machine being used to line a tunnel of the Victoria Water Project in Sri Lanka with concrete. (Balfour Beatty UK)*

WATER IN THE GROUND

There is seven times more water trapped in the ground than in all the lakes and rivers of the world. It is called groundwater and may be running through a layer near the surface after rain, or it may be in the 'zone of saturation' which is always wet. Under this zone there is hard, hot, dry rock which water never reaches.

This saturated ground follows the contours of the land, sometimes surfacing as a swamp or lake, sometimes shooting from a hillside as a spring. At the seaside it is close to the surface, as you know from digging in the sand.

Water is also present underground in rivers, streams and lakes.

For tunnellers, the presence of water creates many problems including flooding tunnels and making the ground unstable.

TUNNEL SHAPES AND SIZES

A circular tunnel deflects pressure best, but a flat bottom may be needed if a circle is not the best shape for the tunnel's purpose. A tunnel carrying two or more traffic lanes or rail tracks, for example, may need to be wider than it is high. Then space is needed to house equipment for ventilating poisonous fumes in road tunnels and for drainage systems in tunnels running through wet ground.

BUILDING A TUNNEL

To build tunnels quickly, as many portals as possible are worked at the same time, one at each end and others from shafts along the route which can later be used for ventilation, thereby reducing the distance which tunnellers and spoil have to travel underground.

To create the tunnel, the ground has to be broken through and removed, the tunnel supported temporarily while being worked, then permanently for use.

As water will almost always continue to seep in, drainage is needed even after the tunnel is finished. After completion, all that is necessary for a particular tunnel has to be put in place; things like lighting, ventilation, road surfaces, railway lines, emergency escape routes, and equipment for dealing with fires and accidents.

METHODS OF EXCAVATION

There are many different kinds of ground but methods of excavation are of two main types, known as 'hard rock' and 'soft ground'.

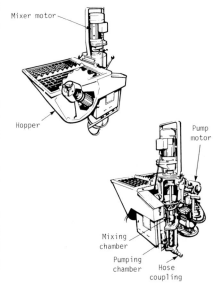

Fig. 9   *Diagrams of a mortar mixing machine developed in Austria which is small enough to be used in a tunnel, making it possible to mix mortar on site. (T&T)*

At the centre of the Earth, about
6000km deep there is a molten iron
and nickel core which is 3000°C.
Even though mine shafts are rarely
deeper than 5km and tunnels are
even closer to the surface, the heat
of the rock and water can still be
overwhelming, because the crust of
the Earth is being constantly
warmed from the molten core.

Within the layers of ground and
in the water which seeps through it,
there are chemicals which erode
and weaken rock. When these
chemicals are released by tunnelling activity they can give off
poisonous and explosive gases.

Fig. 10 *Tunnellers wear ear protection
when they place explosives in the rock. (Nitro
Nobel AB Sweden)*

Hard Rock Tunnelling

The problem with rock is that it is hard to break and carry away, but once a
hole has been made the surrounding rock is often firm enough to form its own
natural arch and needs only strengthening in some places to withstand the
constant squeezing pressure of surrounding rock.

Since the invention of dynamite, rock has been blasted by drilling holes,
filling them with explosives and then blasting. The position of the holes has
traditionally been painted on the rock but now laser illumination is sometimes
used. Detonators ensure the correct timing of explosions and allow tunnellers
to retreat to safety until the charges have been fired, the rock broken, and
poisonous fumes cleared. They then return to remove loose rock and put up
temporary wall and arch supports. Steel arches, metal bolts up to 5m long, and
sprayed concrete can be used. A concrete lining is later put in place as a
permanent shell.

When ground conditions are constant along a reasonable section, a boring
machine is cheaper and faster to use than blasting.

Boring machines either 'eat' the complete circumference of the tunnel and
pass out the rock onto a conveyor, leaving a hole smooth enough for a prefabricated concrete lining to be put in place, or they may be more like the
mechanical diggers we see on building sites which 'nibble' at the tunnel face,
causing the rock to fall onto conveyors.

Soft Ground Tunnelling

The problem with soft ground, (found under most towns and rivers) is
holding back loose material so that it does not fall into the cleared space. For
smaller tunnels, wood or steels struts and netting are sufficient, but in larger
tunnels where pressure from the surrounding ground is greater, movable
shields which also protect tunnel boring machines in soft ground are often
used.

Water, which can turn soil into oozing mud, is particularly troublesome in
soft ground and a number of ways have been developed to control it.
Sometimes excavation is carried out under pressure created by compressed
air. Sometimes the ground ahead of the tunnel is treated with grouts or
chemicals to make it firmer, or it is frozen. Sometimes wells are dug and water
is pumped out of the ground before tunnelling begins.

Variations in the Ground

In practice the division is not quite so clear cut, for tunnellers blasting through
a hard rock mountain may reach a wide, deep fault filled with soft material, or
an underground stream. Tunnellers believing themselves to be safely below
the river bed, may encounter a fault in the rock that connects with the river
bed, which could allow the water from the river to flood the tunnel.

TUNNELLING TECHNOLOGY

Tunnelling technology has benefited from and contributed to the progress of
problem solving through the centuries. The story of this technology is told in
the side panels of the chapters.

2
THE FIRST TUNNELS

Many Stone Age cave dwellers died when tunnels collapsed on them as they tried to extend their caves. But tunnelling had begun. Archaeologists have found their fossilised remains alongside their primitive tools.

At Bomvu Ridge in Swaziland in Southern Africa 40,000 years ago, Neanderthal men burrowed under the ground with bare hands, bones and sharp stones for hematite, a rich red blood stone prized for personal decoration and used in burial rites.

Twenty thousand years ago spearheads were made from flint in Spain and France, then flint tools began to be used in England, Belgium, France and Sweden. These spread more widely and were later replaced by copper, bronze then iron chisels.

Copper smelting was developed by the Sumerians and five thousand years ago copper was extensively mined in Cyprus. Four thousand years ago gold was mined in Peru and salt at Halstadt in Austria. Five hundred years later iron was worked, first in Armenia.

Tunnelling was not always put to positive use. For instance, when people built walls around cities for protection, tunnellers dug under them, hoping to collapse them, like the wall of Jericho in the Bible. In contrast, the Ellora mountain rock temples are hallmarks of creativity. The ornate beauty of Indian carvings appear not in wood, but cut into the face of the rock itself for a distance of more than 10kms. Only hand tools were used for this work.

THE EGYPTIANS

Nubia, in the language of Ancient Egypt, meant goldfield. Over three thousand years ago, mining for gold in the Nubian desert south of Coptos, the world's first gold boom town, allowed Egypt to grow rich enough to dominate the Middle East. Some of the gold in Tutankhamun's tomb came from Coptos. It was mined to a depth of 90m along a 460m seam, using stone hammers and copper tools, while the roof was supported by wooden props. A papyrus map, the oldest mine map in the world, held in Turin museum, shows roads, the gold bearing hills and over a thousand stone miner's huts.

About three thousand years ago massive deposits of copper were excavated from King Solomon's Mines north of Eilat in Israel where Phoenician artisans and over 80,000 slave miners were used.

Emerald mines near the Red Sea reached a depth of 240m, but it was silver, the gift of the Moon God, and gold, the gift of the Sun God, which excited the Egyptians. The Abu Simbel temple was tunnelled over fifty metres into the rock on the orders of Rameses II to honour the Sun God. It was designed so that the sun's rays reached the inner sanctum only twice a year on the 23rd of

EARLY DRAINAGE

Early tunnels were drained by slave-powered waterwheels, or cochleas (invented by Archimedes) each of which raised water by 2m or 3m and had to be used one above the other.

BREAKING HARD ROCK

Breaking up a face of hard rock was done by cutting holes into it, then driving in wooden plugs and wetting them so that they expanded. The holes were cut by one man holding a chisel while a second struck it with a hammer.

Egyptian Fire Setting

The Egyptians were the first to use fire setting, which went on for centuries. Fire at the tunnel face heated the rock so that it expanded, then cold water or vinegar was thrown on so that it contracted and split. Slaves were suffocated by smoke, choked by fumes, and poisoned by escaping gases, but they were considered expendable.

Gunpowder

Gunpowder, which centuries later was used to break up the face, was actually invented in China about the year 250AD but because of the teachings of Confucius about the simplicity of life, tunnelling was spasmodic in China, and mining even prohibited at times, so tunnellers in other parts of the world did not know how useful gunpowder could be.

Fig. 11 (Top left) *Ancient mining was a hit and miss affair. A tunnel was dug into the side of a hill in the hope that it would connect with most of the shafts. If one did connect the miners in the shafts and the tunnellers all worked together, to bring ore to the surface from both shaft and tunnel. If the shaft did not reach the tunnel the miners raised what ore they could from the shaft alone. Men and ore were hoisted out by a hand operated windlass, often shielded from the rain by a hut.*

Fig. 12 (Bottom left) *The only method of removing rubble and water from ancient tunnels was with a bucket attached by rope to a windlass. When the shaft was shallow the wheel was quite small and could be turned by one man. When the shaft was deeper it often took the strength of three men using a windlass of the type shown here to raise the bucket to the surface.*

Fig. 13 (Bottom Right) *Hard rock could not be broken up by tunnellers unless it was heated. To do this logs were shaped by hand cutting on the surface, then carried to the rock face in the tunnels. The heat weakened the rock, but if it still refused to crack, vinegar was thrown onto the hot rock causing it to splinter. The smoke and vinegar fumes created a very nasty mist, from which the tunneller in this picture is shielding his eyes.*

The three illustrations in this section come from – De Re Metallica written by Georgius Agricola in 1556 (British Library)

February and October. When in the 20th Century the building of the Aswan High Dam threatened to submerge the temple it was cut into 30 tonne blocks and moved to the safety of a higher site by Swedish engineers.

Tunnelling expertise was also used to carve out tombs for the Pharaohs, including the tomb of Seti which was over 200m long.

THE GREEKS

The wealth and power of Greece, over 2500 years ago, was built on tunnelling achievement. Over ten million tons of lead with silver in it was mined at Laurium, from land owned by the city state but leased to private citizens, who paid a royalty on the gold and silver extracted. Over two thousand shafts were dug and the ore was excavated using hammers, picks, chisels and iron shovels with wooden handles.

The Greeks were the first organisers of communal water supplies. Athens was supplied by an underground network of clay pipes linked to a reservoir outside the city. One of the greatest Greek water tunnels was built on the island of Samos. A hill stood between the city of Vathy and its water source, and a tunnel over 2m high and broad and over one and a quarter kilometres long was dug to provide water for baths and fountains.

THE ROMANS

The Romans were the world's first large scale civil engineers, constructing mine, road and water tunnels throughout their empire. They built 350km of water supply aqueducts in Rome alone between 312BC and 52AD. While Athens was part of the Roman Empire, Hadrian's Aqueduct was built to supply it with fresh water from underground streams. It was rediscovered in 1840, easily repaired and used until 1925 when it was reconstructed. It still serves the city today.

Among the greatest of Roman projects was the tunnel which drained Lake Fucino. For eleven years, over 30,000 slaves a day dug out a total of a million cubic feet of earth which had to be dragged up one or other of the forty shafts, some as deep as 120m, in copper buckets. But when the 5.6m tunnel was completed it allowed 50,000 acres of land to be used for farming.

The Romans also built a road tunnel almost 1km long through Posilipo Hill outside Naples, and one almost twice that length to drain Alban Lake and prevent the flooding of farmland.

Catacombs were built under Roman cities for the burial of the dead, and when early Christians were persecuted they met secretly in the tunnels which linked them.

ROMANS BUILT STRAIGHT TUNNELS

The Romans were the first to build straight tunnels. They sank shafts along a planned route and excavated between them. Plumb lines were used to maintain correct depths and simple instruments devised to ensure that the tunnel floor was flat.

Previously tunnellers had zigzagged underground, guided only by noises from above. A famous example was King Hezekiah's tunnel in 715BC. Fearing a siege of Jerusalem, he ordered a tunnel to draw water from a pool only 35m away outside the city. The tunnel ran in an S shape for more than twice that length and tunnellers from one end only met those from the other by turning at right angles on hearing the noise of parallel digging.

HOW A MINE WORKS

There are four kinds of mining, alluvial in stream or river bed, surface in quarries, non-entry mining including the sinking of oil wells, and underground mining which involves tunnelling.

An underground mine is begun by sinking a shaft, either straight down or on an incline from the surface, or by cutting an adit into the side of a hill. Cross-cutting tunnels are dug at various levels into the seam from the shaft.

HOW THE TUNNEL IS SUPPORTED

A mine must be safe from collapse at all times, and the level of support necessary to ensure this depends on the stability of the rock and the pressure of it. Wooden posts or pillars, or ore and waste rock, are often used where there is little danger of collapse.

When the Ophir mine was excavated in the USA in the 19th Century the walls were unstable. Philip Deidesheimer developed a modular timber system to give support. These 'Square Sets' are now used in all similar conditions. Where necessary rock bolts, developed in the USA in the 1940s, hold back the walls.

HOW THE AIR IS KEPT FRESH

Before the 19th Century bellows were used to ventilate mines, first hand operated, later powered by a water wheel at the surface.

19th Century coal miners faced 'choke damp', a mixture of nitrogen and carbon dioxide. A ventilating shaft was introduced as an exit for air which had entered by the main shaft. Because hot air rises a

3
TREASURES OF THE EARTH

After the fall of the Roman Empire people in Europe lived in simple isolated communities which were disrupted from time to time by barbaric invasions. But in parts of Britain, Saxony, Bohemia and Spain metals were mined regularly. Mining took place in other parts of the world, including gold mining and smelting in Zimbabwe.

European economic activity was co-ordinated once more under Charlemagne, from 800AD, when gold and silver was demanded for coinage and base metals needed for weapons. Stone, marble, brass and jewels were required for the magnificent churches and cathedrals built at this period.

From 1096 the Crusades opened up trade with the East, weakened feudalism at home as lords sold land to pay for them, and encouraged serfs to prospect as free men for mineral deposits. Through to the 14th Century tunnelling in mines was the springboard for an expanding civilisation. Towns grew in size and some small traders became merchants and bankers.

The Rammelsberg mine in the Harz mountains of Saxony was worked for over 1000 years from 968AD as a leading producer of copper, silver and lead. A silver rush on the slopes of the Erzgebirge mountain in Upper Saxony led to the development of that area. Saxony became rich from mineral resources to be outshone in the late Middle Ages by Bohemia. By this time coal and tin were being excavated in England, coal in Belgium, metals in Austria and copper in Sweden. The miners of Saxony had become so skilled that Venetian merchants asked them to develop mines in Serbia.

THE IMPACT OF CHRISTIANITY

Miners soon became privileged workers, and had to be paid well to undertake the dangerous work because Christianity forbade slavery. In Saxony they were exempt from military service and taxation and formed free associations usually of sixteen members, owing no allegiance to a feudal lord. Their children who worked with them were also deemed to be members.

In Devon and Cornwall miners could prospect anywhere except churchyards, highways, orchards and gardens, paying only a 10% royalty to landowners. Like miners in Derbyshire and elsewhere in England they had their own parliament and courts, and could not be tried outside them.

Medieval miners were conscious of being part of the religious pattern of life and adopted Saint Barbara as their patron. Even today mines and tunnels are dedicated to her and her statue is placed at every portal. Miners and tunnellers in Germany, Poland, France and Italy honour her feast day on

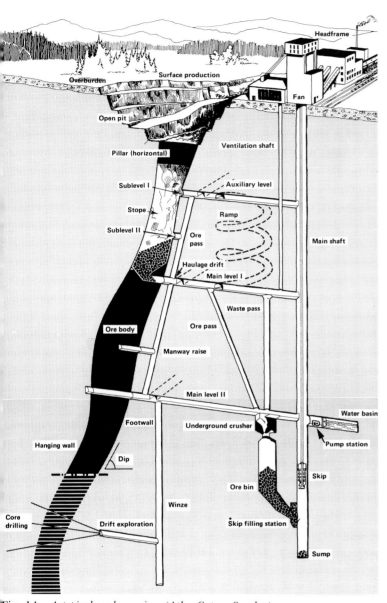

Fig. 14 *A typical modern mine. (Atlas Copco, Sweden)*

Labels in figure: Headframe, Overburden, Surface production, Fan, Open pit, Ventilation shaft, Pillar (horizontal), Sublevel I, Auxiliary level, Stope, Ramp, Sublevel II, Ore pass, Main shaft, Haulage drift, Main level I, Waste pass, Ore pass, Ore body, Manway raise, Main level II, Water basin, Footwall, Underground crusher, Pump station, Hanging wall, Dip, Skip, Ore bin, Winze, Skip filling station, Core drilling, Drift exploration, Sump

December 4th with holidays, music and parades. Legend says that St Barbara was baptised in the 3rd Century against her father's wishes. He beheaded her, and was struck dead by lightning from a cloudless sky.

THE MOVE TOWARDS DEEPER MINES

Medieval mines were often bell pits. A shaft was dug and the area around the bottom excavated to form the shape of a bell. By 1350 many had been worked out and, when Black Death scourged Europe, progress was halted for a hundred years.

brazier was placed at the bottom of many ventilation shafts.

Mechanical ventilators were tried. The first, called a Blow George, needed three men to operate it. In 1835 William Fourness of Leeds invented the first exhaust fan which, together with improved models, was ventilating most mines by 1850.

Ventilation is also needed to clear 'firedamp', an explosive mixture of air and methane gas found mainly in coal mines. Because this is done most safely without naked flames or hot machinery, electricity is now used to power extractor fans.

In the deep gold mines of South Africa where rock temperature reaches 140°F, refrigeration plants have been built underground to cool the air.

HOW A MINE IS LIT

16th Century European miners held slow burning slivers of pine wood in their teeth so as to keep both hands free for work.

In coal mines heat can cause explosions so in the 18th Century lamps with a cool flame were needed. The first used rotting fish skins and bones to produce a phosphorescent glow. In 1760 Carlisle Spedding invented a device which depended on sparks made by hand cranking a steel wheel against a piece of flint. Both systems created flashes of light to which miner's eyes were regularly attracted leading to the disease nystagmus, in which oscillation of the eyeball becomes uncontrollable.

In 1798 Humboldt did manage to invent a safety lamp but it would not burn properly in impure air, and it was not until 1815 that Davy created the first practical safety lamp for gassy mines. The flame in it changed colour so that it could also be used to detect methane.

In mines where explosions were not a problem, oil lamps were replaced by tallow burners and then candles. A chandler was employed in each mine to make the candles, which were either fixed on the rock wall or attached to a miner's hat by a daub of clay. When ventilation improved, gusts of air blew out candles and by 1900 acetylene lamps were the most common form of light.

Electric cap lamps were introduced in 1910 which miners clip to their helmets and connect to batteries on their belts.

At major seams electric lighting is now installed using gas filled incandescent lamps or fluorescent strip lights. When machinery is used at the face it is often illuminated by floodlights and rock walls are painted white to reflect more light.

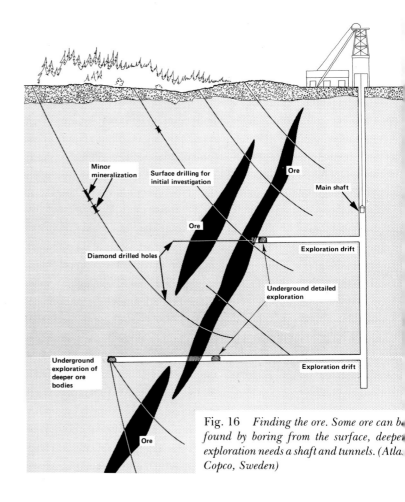

Fig. 16 *Finding the ore. Some ore can be found by boring from the surface, deeper exploration needs a shaft and tunnels. (Atlas Copco, Sweden)*

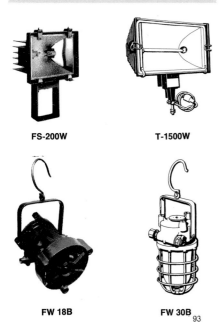

FS-200W **T-1500W**

FW 18B **FW 30B**

Fig. 15 *Explosion proof brass lamps approved for use in methane atmospheres. (Atlas Copco, Sweden)*

Modern mining was started off in 1450 when Johannes Funckel discovered a new way to separate silver from copper, and by the development of the Stockofen furnace in Saxony which tripled the amount of iron which could be smelted from ore.

The deep level mines which were developed in Saxony, Bohemia and Hungary during the next two hundred years required more capital than the miner's associations could command. Companies of 128 absentee share holders were formed and managers appointed so that miners lost their independence and became hired hands.

European mining boomed until the middle of the sixteenth century when the Spanish Conquistadors arrived in South America. They found huge quantities of already mined minerals and then excavated for more, using the natives as cheap captive labour. Thus funded by plundered wealth, European trade and production prospered, but European mining declined and miners lost their privileged position for ever.

COAL AND THE INDUSTRIAL REVOLUTION

Coal mined in Britain began the next European tunnelling revival. At first simply replaced shortages of wood charcoal, but during the 18th Century the

Figs. 17a+b *A roadheader excavator at work in a mining tunnel (above) and a close up of its water jet (below). (Anderson Strathclyde UK)*

HOW THE SEAMS ARE BROKEN UP

Soft rock seams which were previously cut by hand can now be excavated by complex machines, but many of the Earth's treasures lie in hard rock.

Soft Ground Cutters

As early as 1761, William Brown invented a mechanical robot to copy the actions of a man cutting coal. Later a steam powered circular steel disc was tried, then in 1861 Lord Cochrane invented a compressed air coal cutter which was first used in a mine in Wigan, in England in 1868. A chain cutter was developed in 1894 and in the 20th Century electrically powered machinery was introduced.

Continuous mining which removed the need even for hand shovelling into conveyors was introduced into some mines in the USA in the 1940s and into Europe a decade later. Nowadays some seams are worked entirely by mechanical cutters operated by remote control.

Breaking Up Hard Rock

Although the ancient practice of fire setting was still being used in the Rammelsberg mine until 1878, elsewhere it had gradually been replaced by explosives.

At first gunpowder was piled up at the rock face, but this was seen to be wasteful, so holes were drilled and plugged with explosive. The hardest rock could not be drilled by hand and the process was slow on all rock, so during the 19th Century steam powered drills were tried. A major problem was that the drills very quickly got too hot to use. To solve it L G Leyner of Denver USA used a hollow drill in 1897 so that air and water could be forced through the middle of it to cool down both rock and drill and wash away rock cuttings. These wet drills were in common use by 1920, since when compressed air drills, like the ones used for road works, and more recently quieter hydraulically powered drills have been used.

Explosives too have changed. Alfred Nobel's fulminate detonator, introduced in 1867 was the first safe method of igniting high powered explosives. In 1875 he invented nitroglycerine which is still widely used.

Ammonium nitrate is cheaper than nitro and became a viable alternative in 1935 when it could be safely packed in metal cans. In the 1950s a more effective agent ANFO (94% ammonium nitrate, 6% fuel oil) was introduced at a third of the cost of nitro but it would not work in water until in 1960 Dr Cook of Utah University USA perfected ammonium nitrate slurries. Ammonium nitrate based products are now used for three quarters of all blasting.

HOW WATER IS CONTROLLED

When a mine is operated below groundwater level, water continually seeps into the workings. The oldest method of solving this problem dates back over 3000 years to the iron mines at Mitterberg in the Tyrol when a drainage adit was first used. A tunnel was dug into the hillside below mine level and shafts sunk into it from the mine down which the water drained.

Between 1748 and 1800 an adit

use of coal for iron smelting spread from Sweden and Russia to Britain, France, Belgium, Austria and Germany. Then came steam, first used for British machinery in the 1770s, but going on to power the Industrial Revolution across Europe and the newly independent United States of America to the world, bringing with it enormous demands for iron and coal. In 1700 Britain was the world's biggest coal user, burning 3 million tons a year. By 1980 the world was consuming 3000 million tons annually.

Conditions in 19th Century British coal mines were very hard and miners were often bonded to an owner for a year at a time, unable to leave whatever the level of cruelty. Boys as young as five sat in solitude, damp and darkness for twelve hours a day, occasionally opening an air door, until they were big enough to haul coal. In some Scottish mines, girls of six were hired to drag wooden troughs loaded with coal to the surface from dawn to dusk.

In 1842 a law was passed forbidding children under 10 and women from working underground but it was another 40 years before the age limit was increased to 12.

Pits were dangerous places, lung disease was common, and the risk of accident or explosion was constant. In Northumberland in 1862 a heavy engine fell blocking the only shaft and 204 men and boys were suffocated. Between 1891 and 1900 a thousand people died as a result of 38 mine explosions in the USA, and in 1941 in Honkeiko China as many died as a result of just one explosion. Better ventilation has now reduced the chances of such deaths.

Mines became so large in the 19th Century that they dominated whole towns and even areas of a country as generation after generation found them the sole source of employment. Since the development of oil and other forms of energy mining of seams past their prime has become uneconomic and many mining areas have high levels of unemployment. But employed or not, mining communities, through their shared hardships, are among the most close-knit in the world.

Fig. 18   *The Selby Coalfield in Yorkshire. The tunnel on the left of this photograph contains the 12,000 hp motor which drives the conveyor hauling coal from depths of up to 1000m and from as far away as 24km. The coalfield holds 2000 million tons of coal and is the size of the Isle of Wight (British Coal)*

Fig. 19 *This 'river of coal' has stopped temporarily for maintenance work on the conveyor.
(British Coal)*

Coal is still mined in vast quantities for use in industry and as a fuel and in the creation of electricity.

RUSHING FOR GOLD

Metal mining was as vital to the late 18th Century development of South America as coal was to Europe. In 1762 over 30 million dollars worth of silver came from just one Mexican mine, and seams of tungsten and vanadium were also found. Gold and diamonds were found in such profusion in Brazil that only Russia, which experienced a Siberian gold rush in the 1840s, could compete.

But then in 1848 James W. Marshall found specks of gold in rocks while building a sawmill and the California gold rush began. Many prospectors earned twenty times an average day's wages while even luckier ones made fortunes. Gold was found in rivers, streams and shallow ground. After California came Colorado and Nevada then, thanks to Edward Hargreaves who returned empty handed to Australia from the USA in 1850 but determined to find gold at home, New South Wales then Victoria, Queensland and Western Australia. Near the end of the century there were gold rushes in the Canadian Yukon and Alaska.

In each place the prospectors soon picked the surface clean and it was left to professional deep level miners to excavate the bulk of the precious metals. In the Comstock Lode in Colorado tunnellers found as much silver as gold. Nowadays most gold is unearthed by deep level mining and the large scale crushing of ore.

was constructed in Cornwall consisting of thirty miles of tunnels winding over a five mile area and draining 46 mines.

The alternative drainage system is to bring the water up to the surface. Roman methods were used for centuries but in the Middle Ages the rag and chain pump was introduced which was powered by men, horses or a surface water wheel. Rags or cups attached to a metal chain collected water from a sump (a tank at the bottom of the shaft) raised it and discharged it into a trough. In Slovakia three units were used one above the other to drain water from 200m deep. Twenty four horses were used in teams of eight working round the clock at each of the three levels.

In 1631 David Ramsey patented a machine to raise water using steam power, but it was 1712 before Thomas Newcomen built the world's first really useful steam engine to pump water from Dudley Castle coal mine in England. In the second half of the century John Smeaton, James Watt and Matthew Boulton created better steam engines which used less coal and powered the Industrial Revolution.

By 1820 further improvements by Trevithick and Woolf had created a Cornish pump world famous for its simplicity and reliability. One was used at the Burra Burra mine in South Australia to pump two million gallons of water a day until 1877, and the last one only ceased work in Cornwall as recently as 1955.

Electricity now drives pumps which can remove a hundred million gallons of water a day from over 700m down the Konkola mine in Zambia.

HOW COAL AND ORE ARE HAULED

After cutting, ore or coal must be transported to the shaft ready for hoisting out.

Hand hauling of flat bottomed trucks or baskets, some holding as much as 500lbs, was common until the 18th Century when John Curr, manager of a colliery in Yorkshire, England, introduced wooden corves which ran on cast iron wheels. They were known as trams, and some were pulled by pit ponies.

The First Locomotives

The 19th Century was the era of steam and the world's first steam locomotive was built by Richard Trevithick in 1801 for use in coal mines. In 1814 George Stephenson built a steam locomotive for Killingworth Colliery in England and in 1824, the year before the first passenger railway, a steam engine transported over 50,000 tons of ore and 20,000 tons of coal.

The world's first electric locomotive was introduced for mine haulage in 1833, the year before the first street tram appeared in Germany.

Early this century compressed air locomotives were used to haul coal cars. These have now been replaced by electric trolleys and diesel locomotives, or conveyor belts.

DIAMONDS AND SOUTH AFRICA

Until the 18th Century India was the prime source of diamonds, but then Brazil took the lead. The first South African diamonds weren't discovered until 1867, but by 1869 there was already a rush to the Vaal River, and by 1871 the first Kimberley mine was the hunting ground of 3000 individual prospectors. At a depth of 125m cooperation became essential and by 1880 there were just 70 companies sinking shafts to 250m. Deeper working demanded more capital and by 1890 one company, Cecil Rhodes' De Beers, controlled 90% of South African diamond mining, sinking shafts from the surface to a depth of 1000m. Nowadays thirty million ounces of ground are shifted for every ounce of diamond isolated.

Fig. 20 *One operator can run several of these mining drill rigs, because, when it has been positioned, a computer in each controls the work. (Atlas Copco, Sweden)*

Fig. 21   *Remote control allows the tunneller to stand back out of danger.*
(Atlas Copco, Sweden)

Fig. 22   *These hand held carbide tipped steel drills were introduced in the 1950s.*
Many sophisticated machines have been modelled on them since.
(Atlas Copco, Sweden)

Traditionally, in shallow mines rope ladders were used, and for deeper shafts ropes were lowered and hoisted by windlass.

As mines went deeper horses powered whip or whim hoists – the whip involving a straight pull over pulleys – the whim winding the rope around a drum like a giant windlass on its side.

When mines went deeper still, two or three stage hoisting was necessary using chains rather than ropes, and water wheel power was sometimes used.

In 1784 Boulton and Watt invented the steam hoisting machine, which was only moderately successful because the corves twisted and collided and had to be put into heavy iron cages. For the deepest mines the machine could only be used successfully after wire ropes were developed in 1833 in the German Harz mountains.

Since the 1920s electrically driven power hoists have been most common and include those for the deepest South African mines which have the pulling power of 6000 horses.

ORE SEPARATION AND ECONOMIC BENEFITS

In Australia in 1922 work on a refinement process for extracting ore was perfected, clearing the way for construction of the world's largest smelting plant in 1925. Dr G.K. Williams introduced the world's first continuous refining process for the separation of lead from zinc in 1932. As a result of these activities the vast deposits of silver, lead and zinc at Broken Hill in New South Wales could be profitably exploited, and this led to investment in a wide variety of Australian industry.

Fig. 23   *This digging arm can load 6 cubic metres of ore a minute. (Atlas Copco, Sweden)*

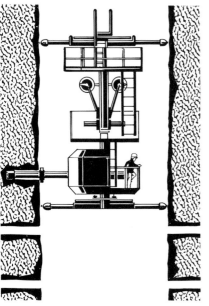

Fig. 24   *Diagram showing how shafts are enlarged by drilling holes radially from a centra[shaft. The holes are charged with explosive and blasted to form a larger shaft. (T&T)*

MINING TODAY

Canada's success in the world owes a lot to the exploitation of its vast range o[mineable resources including uranium, of which it is a leading producer.

Throughout the world precious and base metals and many kinds of rock ar[extracted from the ground and turned into products we can all enjoy.

So vast is today's mining industry that by the year 2000 it is expected tha[over 42,000km of new mining tunnels will be dug each year in the USA alone[

But this level of activity and its benefits are not achieved without dangers t[the environment. It is now possible to remove the earth's treasures at such [speed that some scientists fear we will use up the Earth's limited resources to[quickly and create shortages for the future.

Fig. 25   *A roadheader inside a shield is being lowered into a shaft to dig a sewer tunnel. (Mowlem UK)*

4

UNDERPINNING CIVILISATION

Tunnels help to underpin civilisation by carrying communication systems and essential supplies of water. But in a way they also reflect the values of communities. The road and aqueduct tunnels of the Romans indicated the kind of society in which their subjects lived, just as the new tunnels of Europe which followed Rome's decline indicated the values of those times. In the main they were simple, providing water for monasteries and manor houses and, as towns grew in size, bringing them water on the 'village well and parish pump' scale.

One of the few complex underground networks was built under Moscow for Ivan the Terrible. It included dungeons and torture chambers and even a

DRILLING JUMBOS

The drilling jumbo used to divert the waters of the Colorado River USA early this century was a platform on which 45 men stood to operate 30 rock drills.

By 1983 the jumbo used to drill the holes for blasting to divert the Leach River in Canada for Victoria's water supply was a sophisticated hydraulic machine. The contractor for that scheme was Grizzly Rock Services.

Fig. 26 (Top) *An electric train pulling equipment along a water tunnel during construction. (Spie Batignolles, France)*

Fig. 27 (Centre) *View up a shaft lined with pre-cast concrete sections. (Buchan UK)*

Fig. 28 (Bottom) *Lining a water tunnel with pre-cast concrete. (Charcon Tunnels UK)*

tunnel which led out to a forest full of wild beasts. These were tempted into the network so that Ivan could watch them killing and eating people.

But as modern civilisation developed so did the tunnel networks.

WATER SUPPLY

It was only after the Industrial Revolution that shortage of water and the technology to build deep level tunnels to supply it in quantity coincided.

The authorities of Liverpool flooded a valley over 100km away, obliterating an entire village in the process; those of Manchester tapped into the Lake District and, later, the people of Birmingham drew their supplies from Wales.

In America in 1867 the citizens of Chicago, in need of water, looked out over Lake Michigan, which was polluted by sewage and shipping, and decided to divert their sewage elsewhere. Then they built tunnels 3km out into the drinkable waters of the lake. But their endeavour was not without risk. Sixty men were killed when a temporary crib over a shaft 2km from shore caught fire, burning some to death and suffocating others who fled down the shaft.

New York in its search for water had an underground aqueduct built from Croton Lake to Central Park Reservoir. This was completed in 1891, but within twenty years New Yorkers needed to tap into the Catskill mountains, an exercise which had to be repeated to deeper levels in the 1930s. At this time San Franciscans were tunnelling over 300km into the Sierras for their supplies and other Californians needed to reach the Colorado River 600km away for theirs. When Cleveland tunnellers under Lake Erie used canaries to test for poisonous air they were reported to the local Humane Society, but it decided that the practice was justified because it saved human lives.

London's water supply is in cast iron pipes near the surface and there are plans to replace it with new 2.5m diameter tunnels 80m underground. But such replacement is by no means easy. For instance, a reservoir next to the famous Sacré Coeur church in Montmartres, Paris, has supplied water through shallow pipelines for decades, but because the ground under the Sacré Coeur has crumbled, new deep level tunnels are necessary and care has to be taken to preserve the foundations.

IRRIGATION

Many parts of the earth do not get enough rain to make them fertile, and irrigation schemes involving tunnels are necessary. Parts of the USA have been irrigated for a hundred years, but few schemes sprung the surprise which met those tunnelling to irrigate the Colorado desert through the Gunnison Tunnel. When they passed through a rock fault, 5 million gallons of water a day flooded in from an underground river, proving that supplies were available but making tunnelling very difficult.

Saudi Arabia has a Red Sea coast and the Tihama mountains which have chilling temperatures and thick fogs for most of the year. A 102km tunnel and pipeline now link them, taking water from a desalination plant on the coast to the Abha reservoir 2300m higher which can hold 100,000 cubic metres of water to supply the desert country.

West Pakistan's agriculture used to depend on unregulated river flows which led to regular crop failures. In the 1960s the Mangla Dam was built and a network of irrigation tunnels now flows from the lake behind it.

The Victoria Dam in Sri Lanka has created storage of 722 million cubic metres of water. Its effects on the country are enormous. 40,000 people had to move out of its way, but enough farming land had been created for 50,000 people to work it. The cost of £186 million was partly met by £100 million of British aid, and British companies undertook much of the work.

To supply irrigation and industrial water to the Eastern Cape Province of South Africa, an 82km tunnel known as the Orange-Fish tunnel was needed. When the project was discussed in 1962, a 30 year construction period was estimated, but work started in 1968 was finished by 1975 and the tunnel was then the longest in the world.

Tunnellers do not always make the progress they hope for, however. In the 1930s it was decided to irrigate south east Spain by bringing water from the Tagus River, but a tunnel was not completed until the 1980s and because there were over 300 rock faults along the 32km route progress was difficult. In one accident a boring machine was buried which took two years to retrieve.

DRAINAGE AND SEWERAGE

When populations reach a certain size it becomes essential to have drainage systems which prevent flooding and adequate sewage tunnels to prevent disease. But what is that number? Although Henry III ordered water pipes and a Bill of Sewers was passed in the reign of Henry VIII, London still relied on 200,000 cess pits when its population reached a million in 1810.

It was Edwin Chadwick who, during the 19th Century, campaigned actively for tunnelled drainage. In a report compiled by doctors following a cholera epidemic in Leeds in 1842 he wrote, 'In the badly cleansed and drained wards mortality is nearly double that in better conditioned districts.' Partly as a result of that report the first drainage system was constructed in the 1850s, and there followed 60 years of active sewer building in Britain. Only recently have

Fig. 29 *This tunnel built under Carsington reservoir dam is one of the longest in England using standard bolted segments of concrete. (Buchan UK)*

BUILDING AND REPAIRING SEWER TUNNELS

Sinking shafts in busy roads is expensive and inconvenient. Since the 1950s the Japanese have developed remote controlled automatic boring machines protected by shields. They can tunnel in straight lines and around sharp curves.

Nowadays if a sewer pipe is clogged by rubble or even tree roots it can be cleared by water jets, without anyone going underground. Automatic equipment controlled from a van works on the surface between two manholes. Sewers can also be repaired in this way by using chemical grout or polyethylene linings.

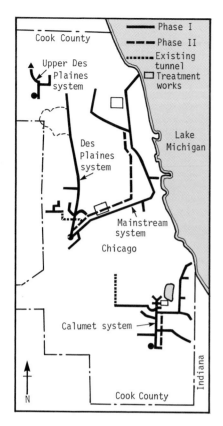

Fig. 30 *Map of the Chicago, USA, Tunnel & Reservoir Plan known as TARP which cost 1200 million dollars. (T&T)*

Fig. 31 *Root clearing by water jet. (T&T)*

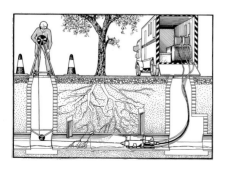

we begun to notice the problems of neglect. In 1980 a double decker bus collapsed into the sewer in a main shopping street in Manchester, highlighting the state of the network.

In the Midwest of the USA many sewer systems were rebuilt in the 1930s, but they were only designed to cope with conservative estimates of population growth and to last for 50 years. In the meantime much has happened to weaken them. Over one shallow tunnel a four lane highway carrying heavy trucks has shaken the concrete for years. Tree roots grew through many of the joints in a tunnel built beneath a forest. A third sewer was found to be blocked by silt because it hadn't been cleaned properly for 60 years.

Sewerage is being improved in many places. For centuries sewage from Bristol in England's West Country has flowed untreated down the Avon to the sea, but during the past 25 years tunnels have been constructed to take 95% of it to a treatment plant, so now the river, including the Bristol floating harbour, can be developed for safe leisure pursuits. New York has ordered over 6000m of new combined sewage and storage tunnels.

The grandest scheme of all in recent years has been the Chicago Tunnel and Reservoir Plan (TARP) which will have 211km of tunnels when complete. Placed 50m underground they will intercept the flow from over 8000kms of existing sewers and store it in reservoirs for treatment and pumping back. Since the first stage was completed in 1985 the scheme has proved its worth. During its first winter over 1000 million gallons of excess flow was stored in 50km of deep tunnels until treatment plants could cope with it. Without it this sewer and storm water would have poured into Lake Michigan.

Many cities have relied on the sea to wash away their sewage but are now needing to have second thoughts. Sewage from Helsinki in Finland has traditionally been poured in to the bay, but there is now too much to be washed away so it will be treated centrally then pumped to the edge of the open sea in the Gulf of Finland through a new tunnel system. Untreated Istanbul sewage has tainted the glorious waterways of the Golden Horn and Bosphorus for centuries, but thanks to two 1km tunnels and financial aid from the World Bank, treated sewage will be carried out to the Marmara Sea. In anticipation of problems with sewage when the Junk Bay development in the Hong Kong New Territories is opened to welcome the first 170,000 of a projected 250,000 people, a tunnel is being constructed to take sewage beyond the bay out into the Tathong Channel. Although such actions are good for the cities they serve, some ecologists are worried that we may be polluting our seas to the point where life on Earth could be threatened.

Cities must have adequate systems. In Egypt, for example, the British built a system for under a million people in Cairo. The city now has twelve million and is expected to house sixteen million by the end of the century. Three million have no sewerage system and only about a third is treated. As a result a higher proportion of babies die in Cairo each year than in most other cities. Now international aid funds have been made available for a network of sewage tunnels.

TUNNELS FOR POWER SUPPLY

The tunnels which supply our power are not all under city streets. In 1982, the Norwegians built three tunnels totalling 12km to bring North Sea gas ashore. The Hjeltefjorden oil tunnel is 10km long and up to 500m below sea level.

TUNNELS FOR HYDRO-ELECTRICITY

Most plants creating nuclear power need some underground tunnelling but the tunnellers' main contribution to power generation has been in the construction of hydro-electric plants.

Sweden produces the majority of its power by hydro-electricity and has been building underground plants since 1910 including some within the Arctic Circle.

Tunnellers working on the Big Creek hydro project in Southern California from 1911 to 1929 were often snowed in 2000m above sea level, and relied on sled-dog teams to communicate with the nearest town. As work progressed further into the mountain a railway line was constructed to transport materials. The train boasted the world's first dining car on a tunnel railway. More recently in Northern California over 20km of tunnels were needed to produce 200MW of peak capacity power.

All of Norway's electricity is hydro-generated, but building plants has not been without problems. The largest power station at Eidfjord suffered many rockbursts during construction in the late 1970s. Eventually over 20,000 bolts with a combined length of over 100km were needed to hold back the rock. When they decided to dam a mountain valley inside the Arctic Circle and build a power station within the mountain, access was possible at first only by helicopter, then by the construction of a 1.2km spiral tunnel. Even in such a desolate area tunnellers worked within tight environmental guidelines which included special measures to protect the salmon in the area. Despite all of these activities, the electricity supply on the west coast of Norway is insufficient for one of Europe's largest producers of aluminium, so the company is building its own hydro plant which will include a 1500m high pressure shaft and 25km of tunnels.

Even in the 1980s old and new come together in sharp contrast when tunnellers go off the beaten track to build hydro stations. In 1983 construction to tap an Alaskan lake included the highest vertical pressure shaft in the USA, but tunnellers lived in old logger's cabins and had to wait for supplies to arrive by barge from Seattle.

Fig. 32 (Above left) *Groundwater under Cairo is very close to the surface, so sewer builders have to work in compressed air. Here three shafts are being sunk to create a large enough area to launch a tunnelling machine. (Edmund Nuttall UK)*

Fig. 33 (Above right) *Cable and telephone apparatus was put into this tunnel under Edinburgh, Scotland. The tunnel has steel arch rib supports. (Mowlem UK)*

Fig. 34 *A French pre-cast concrete conduit, 2m in diameter, for water tunnels. (T&T)*

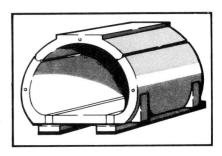

In the 1970s it was decided that Britain needed a pumped-storage hydro-electricity scheme, not just to increase the availability of power but to have a supply which could be quickly activated to meet peak demand. The station was located under the Snowdonia National Park in North Wales. When power is needed water is released from the lake at the top. When demand is low the water is pumped back up to the lake.

Similar schemes have followed in the French Alps, the South African Drakensburgs and under the Nikko National Park to supply Tokyo, Japan.

Hydro-electricity is now being generated all around the world, but for tunnellers working in remote places where proper site investigation has been impossible, the blueprints may become useless. 'What we are doing now looks nothing like the original design,' said a project manager high in the Andes mountains of Columbia in 1986. Yet work is progressing to create a 1600MW capacity hydroelectric scheme, the largest in Colombia with the biggest underground machine hall in the world and, at 550m, the deepest underground power house. The difficult conditions are highlighted by the fact that no road connects the dam site with the powerhouse area.

Fig. 35   *The power cavern of the Gitaru hydro-electric project in Kenya, 1977. (Balfour Beatty UK)*

Fig. 36   *A drilling jumbo at work on a tailrace tunnel for the Gitaru hydro-electric project in Kenya, 1977. (Balfour Beatty UK)*

TUNNELS FOR WAR

We live in a world of competing nations and competing political ideologies. It is hardly surprising, then, that tunnellers build underground defence shelters, or that the USA is studying the use of deep shafts from which rockets can be fired; or that Russia is said to be building coastal caverns at Vladivostok to hide nuclear warships from satellite observation.

The history of many nations has included tunnels and underground networks as part of defence systems but none have been as significant as those of the Viet Cong in the war in Vietnam. From 1960 onwards Vietnamese guerillas dug over 200km of tunnels around Cu Chi, connecting villages from Saigon to the Cambodian border. In these they slept, stored rice and explosives, and set up hospitals. The tunnels included air raid shelters which were cone shaped to amplify the sound of approaching aircraft. Each entrance was a concealed trap door protected by an armoured guard. From these tunnels the Viet Cong eventually drove the US Army from Saigon.

Fig. 37 *A high pressure water pipe for the hydro-electric project in Kenya. (Balfour Beatty UK)*

Fig. 38 *A World War II British air raid shelter tunnel. (Charcon Tunnels UK)*

TUNNELS FOR SCIENCE

The advance of civilisation depends on the search for knowledge and the frontiers of knowledge are being breached by Stanford University in the USA and at CERN, the European organisation for nuclear research. Both these organisations are using tunnel circles, or caverns, in which sub atomic particles collide. The CERN circle which straddles the border between France and Switzerland has a 27km circumference. In America there is now a lobby pressing for the building of a 'superconducting super-collider' using a cavern which at 96km would be big enough to circle Greater London. In it sub-atomic particles would be smashed together in experiments to try to recreate conditions which existed at the earliest moments in the history of the universe.

EMERGENCY AID FOR CIVILISATION

When a massive landslide in the USA in 1963 formed itself into a dam 67m high, 274m wide and 457m thick, water quickly built up behind it creating an unstable lake holding 3700 cubic metres of water. It threatened to fall on towns and roads and block a vital east-west railway route.

Tunnellers worked to divert the water, then cut through the rock to provide an alternative rail route. The residents of Spanish Fork Canyon in Utah had no doubt that tunnellers had preserved civilisation as they knew it.

Fig. 39   *The superconducting super collider, the world's largest physics machine, planned for the USA. (T&T)*

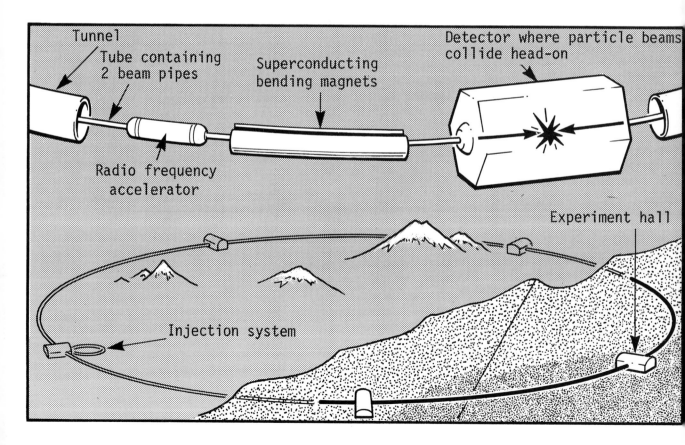

PHOTOFEATURE

Fig. 40   *High in the mountains of Sri Lanka a drilling jumbo is being prepared for work on the Victoria dam in 1981.*

Fig. 41   *By 1983 work was well under way on the dam's downstream portal. (Both photographs Edmund Nuttall UK)*

Fig. 42   Marchlyn dam holds enough water to allow Dinorwig power station in North Wales to generate 1680MW of electricity for five hours. (CEGB UK)

Fig. 43   Water rushes down these smoothly lined tunnels at up to 420 cubic metres per second to create electricity at Dinorwig power station under Snowdonia National Park. (CEGB UK)

Fig. 44 *The valve galleries of the Dinorwig power station. (CEGB UK)*

Fig. 45   *Lower site of the Dinorwig power station in North Wales. (CEGB UK)*

Fig. 46   *Lining a tunnel for a hydro-electric plant in Indonesia. (Balfour Beatty UK)*

Fig. 47 Upper layer of a cavern under construction (top). Lower layer (below). Excavation and tunnel lining (over page top). All for underground power stations. (SGI Switzerland)

Fig. 48 *An access road to a Swiss underground power station. (SGI Switzerland)*

5
THE STORY OF CAVERNS

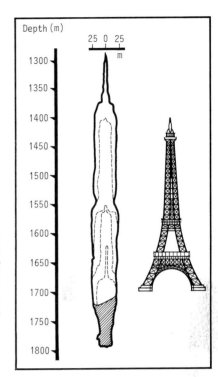

Fig. 49 *Shape and size of a cavern carved into salt which is used to store compressed gas. Compare the size with the Eiffel tower. (T&T)*

Almost 2000 years ago in the Cappodocia area of Turkey people lived in underground communities. Near Aksaray, early Christians carved homes into more than 4000 caves and created a hundred churches in rock using simple hand tools. At Goreme, wind and water erosion created 'Fairy Chimneys' of towering cones and valleys which people cut to create homes. Underground towns at Kaymakli reached 90m down providing up to 20 levels of homes, ceremonial halls and storage space.

MAN MADE CAVERNS OF TODAY

Today Kaymakli has been developed to provide housing, mushroom plantations, and vast storage areas for food which is kept cool by refrigerated ventilation. In other parts of the world tunnellers have excavated caverns in hard rock for the storage of heat sensitive foods such as ice cream.

NEW USES FOR OLD MINES

Many mines of the 19th Century have been converted into storage areas of the 20th. In Southern Belgium, worked out collieries are now used to store reserves of natural gas. A disused iron mine at May-Sur-Orme in France is now an oil store. In Germany 120,000 tons of waste material have been poured into mined-out potash deposits. In Sweden one part of an iron ore mine is still worked actively while the old seams have been converted to ore processing plants, railway yards and storage areas for finished products. Old limestone mines up to 60m below Kansas USA are used as warehouses and factories and cost less than surface buildings. Mine workings in New York and Pennsylvania USA are used to store vehicles. business records and even pleasure boats.

NEW CAVERNS TO STORE ENERGY

Caverns to store oil have been constructed in many countries. Canadians have estimated that their territory has enough suitable sites for 90 million barrels of oil. But it is in Finland that most work has been done on oil storage. The country has no oil of its own and tankers can only bring supplies across the Baltic Sea for eight months a year. Since 1965 at one site alone 35 caverns have been built to hold over five million cubic metres of fuel.

Natural gas and liquid petroleum gas (LPG) are stored in caverns in

MAN MADE CAVERNS

Caverns are usually created in hard rock because soft ground would squeeze in to fill such a large space unless very strong linings were built. The need for such support usually makes soft ground caverns very expensive.

A typical cavern may be 20m high, 15m wide and between 50m and 100m long. For the sake of stability larger caverns are avoided whenever possible and if more space is needed separate caverns are built and linked by tunnels.

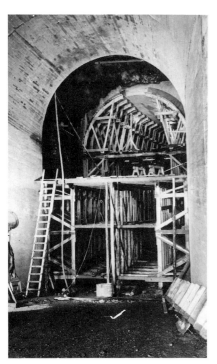

Fig. 50 *This photograph shows one part of a Swiss cavern already lined, and the formwork in place to line the next part. (SGI Switzerland)*

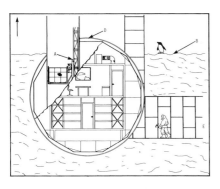

Fig. 51 *Plywood caverns buried under the Antarctic ice cap, in which scientists survive temperatures of −50°C. They are reached by shafts fitted with hoists. (T&T)*

Scandinavia, the USA and Japan where the caverns must be strong enough to survive earthquakes. At Killingholme in Humberside, England, £20 million was spent in the early 1980s on 3km of tunnels to provide cavern storage for £30 million worth of LPG in unlined caverns under desolate flatlands. Refrigerated ground level storage would probably have cost twice as much.

STORAGE FOR NUCLEAR WASTE

Some kinds of nuclear waste will only cease to be dangerous when they have been stored for 100,000 years. A Swedish man-made cave is claimed to have been designed with that life span, while allowing for the reprocessing of fuel rods after 200 years. It is designed to be constructed 200m to 500m below the surface, and each cave will hold between six months' and a year's typical waste from a European country. In Canada plans to create storage areas up to 2000m below the surface are under consideration. It is essential that waste does not escape into the biosphere and specially created caverns are now seen as safer than alternatives such as dumping at sea.

CAVERNS UNDER CITIES

The 10 million cubic metres of caverns under Stockholm, Sweden, were originally built as fall out shelters but have been utilised to store petrol, sand for icy roads, food and hot water. Water purification and sewage treatment plants have been constructed in some of the caverns.

In Norway the construction of air raid and fall out shelters is still being regularly carried out, but now they are designed to double as swimming pools and recreation halls.

The largest underground sports centre in the world is in the Oslo suburb of Holmlia. Its 6500 square metres of space includes courts for volleyball, handball and basketball, a swimming pool and sauna, gymnasium and shooting gallery.

LIVING UNDERGROUND

It is claimed that in China a great many underground homes were built at the height of fears of nuclear attack and that these are now used as hotels.

Certainly tunnellers and underground building designers now have the capability of creating large scale underground communities, where people could live protected from the extremes of heat and cold of the surface. People with bronchial and asthmatic disorders would find such controlled environments easier places to live in as medical research in Russia and China has shown.

But whether it would be good in other ways for people to live for long periods underground, and whether they would choose to unless the surface was devastated are questions to which we do not know the answers.

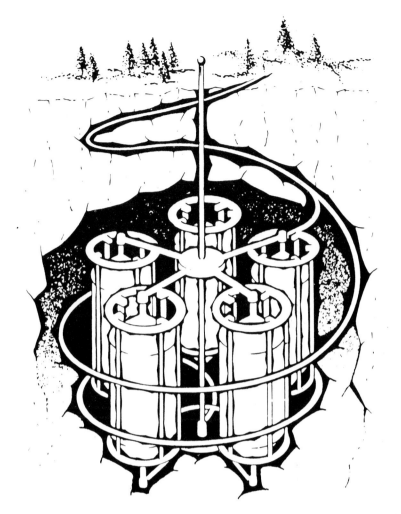

Fig. 52 *A new method of storing oil underground has been devised in Sweden. It is called a Polytank and is made up of five connected vertical shafts 60m in diameter and over 100m high. (T&T)*

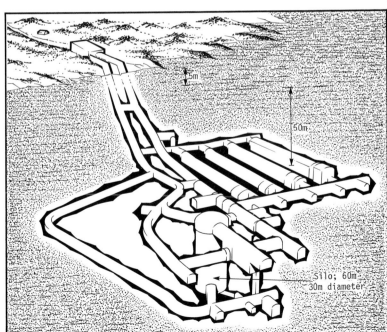

Fig. 53 *This large network of caverns, was used to construct the Forsmark nuclear power station in Sweden. The silo alone measures 30m × 60m. (T&T)*

Silo; 60m
30m diameter

Fig. 54 *A temporary ventilation tube takes air to tunnellers (above) and travellers will cross from one line to another using these tunnels (below) on the Hong Kong Metro. (Mass Transit Railway Corporation, Hong Kong)*

Fig. 55 *Diagram to show how the underpinning of a block of flats made it possible to dig a tunnel for the Singapore Mass Rapid Transit (MRT) without disturbing more than eight families and a coffee shop. (T&T)*

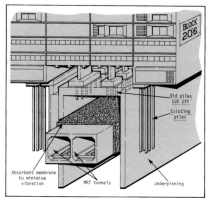

6
TUNNELS
FOR TRANSPORT

The first modern transport tunnel was the Malpas on the Languedoc Canal. It was blasted between 1679 and 1681 to link the Atlantic coast of France with the Mediterranean Sea, an important connection as most goods were carried by river or sea at the time.

18th CENTURY CANAL TUNNELS

For over a century, canals were the unchallenged highways for trade. Work on them was responsible for the development of Civil Engineering as a profession, and of the 'navvy' system of itinerant gangs of labourers who numbered 70,000 in England alone by 1800, most of them Scottish Highlanders or Irish.

When the Bridgewater canal was completed to carry coal from the mines to the city of Manchester in 1761, it improved supply so much that the price of coal was cut by half. Eventually 64km of the canal network was tunnelled underground.

Its designer and builder, James Brindley, was a self-taught individualist who many thought mad because of the daring of his schemes. He had an amazing way of solving complicated tunnelling problems. He examined the difficulties carefully then went to bed, sometimes for three days at a time. He emerged with a detailed solution carefully worked out in his head which he proceeded to put into action without plans or models.

Brindley was also in charge of the Grand Trunk Canal which linked the rivers Mersey, Trent and Severn. This involved the building of a tunnel over 2.5km long through the Harecastle Ridge, which many people considered impossible. When work was started in 1766, windmills and watermills were used to power the drainage pumps, but these proved to be inadequate and work had to be stopped until a Newcomen engine could be fitted. Progress was often restricted to under 1km a day by the conditions and the tunnel took 11 years to build. It had no towpath and 'leggers' had to lie on their backs on the barges and put their feet up onto the tunnel wall to propel the barges through the tunnel, a process which took two hours.

English canals are not usually used to transport goods nowadays, but recently the Blisworth tunnel, originally opened in 1805 on the Grand Junction canal in Northamptonshire was completely refurbished for leisure use.

In a similar way the Lebanon tunnel on the Union canal in the USA is now a national monument. It is the oldest surviving American canal tunnel and was built in 1826.

19th CENTURY RAIL TUNNELS

1826 was the beginning of the decline of canals as the prime movers of goods, not because the world's first railway tunnel, the Terrenoir, was opened in France, that was for horse drawn trains, but because work started in Liverpool in Northwest England, to allow the steam railway to travel underground via the Wapping tunnel.

A visitor who was lowered down a shaft of the Wapping in a bucket reported, 'Numerous candles are burnt by workmen busy with hammer, chisel and pick axe. The frequent blasting of the rock mingles with the hoarse-sounding voices of the miners.'

Over 11,000 kms of railway line were built in the British Isles between 1825 and 1850 and by the end of the century over 50 of the tunnels built were longer than 1.5km.

Three of these were on the London to Birmingham line built by George Stephenson in the 1830s. Construction of one of the three, the Kilsby, resulted in the death of 26 men, and an 8 month delay when tunnellers plunged into quicksand which had not been discovered by the trial borings. Over 1200 navvies were resident for lengthy periods and had to sleep 16 to a room in 4 beds. Two men shared each bed while two others worked for 8 hours and vice versa. The men were well fed, being given plenty of beef to eat.

Stephenson was aware of adverse comments about travel in tunnels which were not well ventilated and became unpleasant because of the smell from burning coke. So when the Primrose Hill tunnel was completed he invited two doctors, two surgeons and a lecturer in chemistry to ascertain the probable effects of the tunnel on the health and feelings of passengers. They reported the tunnel to be of agreeable temperature and free from smell and, being of the opinion that it offered no danger, detriment to health or unpleasantness to travellers, signed their names to those views.

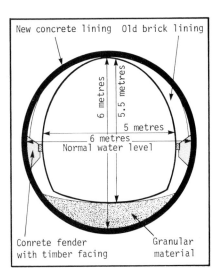

Fig. 56 *A diagram of the inside of part of the Blisworth canal tunnel which shows the old and the new tunnel lining (T&T)*

Fig. 57 *A photograph, taken in 1910, showing a narrow boat emerging from the Crick Tunnel on the Grand Union Canal, having been 'legged' through. (British Waterways Board)*

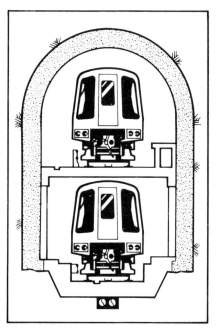

Fig. 58 *In the 1980s this 52 year old railway tunnel was renovated to carry two tracks for the Vancouver Metro, one on top of the other. (T&T)*

Fig. 59 *Timber slats in steel arches provide temporary support during building of a Hong Kong Metro tunnel. (MTRC Hong Kong)*

When Isambard Kingdom Brunel started to build the Box tunnel near Bath, almost 3km long on a 1:100 gradient it was considered dangerous and impractical. Opponents suggested that, 'the train would emerge with a load of corpses, and even if the journey did not prove fatal, no passengers would go twice,' and that, 'if the brakes failed as the train entered the tunnel it would emerge at 120mph,' a rate at which it was claimed, 'no human being could breathe.' Yet the Box tunnel was built by 4000 men and 390 horses working round the clock in such appalling conditions created by explosions, fumes and damp air that over 100 men died during the 5 years of construction. When the service started, some passengers found the prospect of a dark journey accompanied by sparks shooting from the locomotive and sulphurous fumes too frightful to contemplate, so they left the train at the station before the tunnel, and caught the next one from the station after it.

When the Totley tunnel (1888–93) was built for the Manchester–Sheffield line water in the ground presented such problems that the Manchester Guardian reported, 'Every man seemed to possess the miraculous power of Moses, for whenever a rock was struck, water sprang out of it.'

During the 19th Century railway lines were built wherever in the world there were large enough towns to merit a station, and the desire existed to travel or transport goods between them. By 1901, Chicago USA even had an intricate system of underground freight trains. The first American railroad tunnel was the Allegheny Porterage Tunnel (1831–33) in Pennsylvania, one of only 48 transport tunnels in existence in the USA in 1850. But by 1870 America had over 300 tunnels for railways alone.

METRO TUNNELS FOR CITIES

The 19th Century also saw the start of a trend which is still accelerating today, the underground passenger railway for travel in cities and their suburbs.

The world's first underground was the Paddington–Farringdon St line in London. By 1950, sixteen other cities had undergrounds and since then over sixty have been built or commissioned.

Fig. 60 *Woodhead twin track railway tunnel under the English Pennines. (Balfour Beatty UK)*

Fig. 61   *A cross-over tunnel under construction for London Underground's Piccadilly line. (Mowlem UK)*

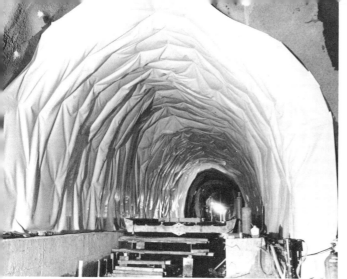

Fig. 62 (Top left) *The New Austrian Tunnelling Method combined with a PVC 'raincoat', to keep out groundwater, was first used in the US on the Washington metro in the 1980s.*

Fig. 63 (Top right) *Platform of the recently constructed Pimlico station in London. (Balfour Beatty UK)*

Fig. 64 (Left) *A crane operated lift and a stairway were alternative ways of travelling down the shaft during construction of the Washington metro. (Both photographs by Phil Portlock for Washington MATA)*

Fig. 66 *The Dartford Tunnel, England 1980. (Balfour Beatty UK)*

Fig. 65 *A view through the protective shield to the tunnel face during construction of the Dartford tunnel. (Balfour Beatty UK)*

ROAD TUNNELS

Since the 1950s the car has replaced the train as the favourite family transport, and freight-carrying lorries have increased in size and number. This has resulted in the building of thousands of road tunnels throughout the world.

Norway is an interesting example of a road building nation. The cost of its tunnels has been kept down by building many of them without linings, taking advantage of the suitable ground, choosing routes carefully and blasting smoothly.

In the far north of Norway beyond the Arctic Circle where it is dark almost all day in winter and light almost all night in summer there is an island called Varda which is inhabited by a fishing community of about 4000 people. Until 1982 it could be reached only by ferry. But then Norwegians built a tunnel 2.8km long, of which 1.7km is under the sea to provide an all weather link with the mainland. Each end of the tunnel has a 100m long portal to prevent snow blocking the entrances.

Fig. 67 *A view through the kind o*
tunnel we take for granted in our town
and cities. This one is the Fort Reger
tunnel on the Island of Jersey. (Edwi
Nuttall UK)

Fig. 68 *A roadheader was designe*
especially to drive this 12m wide tunne
through chalk for the Lewes by-pass
England. (Mowlem UK)

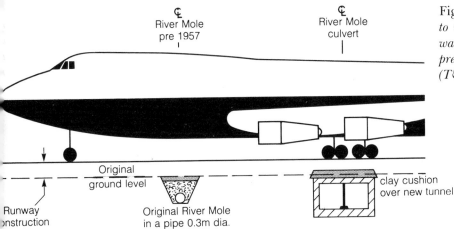

River Mole
pre 1957

River Mole
culvert

Original
ground level

clay cushion
over new tunnel

Runway
construction

Original River Mole
in a pipe 0.3m dia.

Fig. 69   *When heavy aircraft began to use Gatwick Airport, a new tunnel was needed to divert the River Mole and prevent flooding of the runways.* (*T&T*)

20th CENTURY RAIL TUNNELS

Many of our old railway tunnels still serve us well. For instance, when a tanker spilled petrol and started a fire which lasted for three days in a tunnel in northwest England in 1985, the 144 year old brick tunnel lining survived. Some people are convinced that the age of the train is returning. In Germany a decision was taken in the 1960s to update the network. The plan includes a new 327km high speed line between Hanover and Wurzburg only a third of which is at ground level, with one third over bridges and one third underground. In Italy and many other countries the rail network is being updated.

FREIGHT TUNNELS

All over the world tunnels are still being built to allow freight to be carried. In Canada a new Rocky Mountain railway will carry coal 129km to the coast for export to Japan. In Southern Africa, the Isangoyana tunnel is just one of 14 on the coal route from the Transvaal to Richards Bay which will increase the carrying capacity of the line from 21 to 65 million tons of South African coal a year. There are many tunnels on the 3500km single track railway close to the Arctic Circle which has been built by the Russians to exploit the Siberian reserves of gold, oil, gas, coal, lead and copper.

TUNNELS FOR AIR TRAVEL

Even airlines need tunnels, and there are less obvious airport tunnels than the ones we drive under to reach the terminals. For instance a tunnel was needed to divert the River Mole to prevent flooding at Gatwick Airport which serves London. When the 567 tonne Boeing 747s started to rumble along the runways, drainage tunnels needed considerable strengthening.

45

Fig. 70 *The Sommeiller boring machine used on the Mont Cenis tunnel. (Science Photo Library UK)*

7
MOVING MOUNTAINS

SOMMEILLER USES TECHNOLOGY

Germain Sommeiller sought inventions to speed the building of the Mont Cenis tunnel. Drilling holes for explosives by hand was slow so he introduced a percussion drill developed by Joseph Fowle from a design by J J Crouch. Sommeiller himself devised a tube to supply the compressed air necessary for the drill which was generated 800m away. He also invented carriages which could be wheeled up to the rock face with drills mounted on them that made 80 holes at a time. He commissioned Raymond Leschot to devise a hard headed diamond drill to make the holes even faster.

Sommeiller also included into the completed tunnel a ventilation system which depended on water-powered fans, forcing air through an exhaust duct at the top of the tunnel.

Until the middle of the 18th Century the great mountain chains such as t European Alps and the American Rockies stood in the way of travelle Routes over them, if they existed at all, were difficult to cross in summer, a often impassable in winter.

Piercing the Alps had long been a dream. In the 15th Century a road tunn had been started to link Nice with Genoa but never completed. In 184 however, the age of the steam train had arrived and a line was planned to li the North Sea with the Adriatic through Hamburg and Trieste. To do it, t Semmering Railway would need 15 tunnels through the Lower Alps, t longest of which was just under 1km.

But to pierce the Central Alps a 12km tunnel would be needed, starting each end it would have to meet deep in the mountain after the clearance hundreds of thousands of tons of hard rock. At the time no tunnel in t world was a third of this length. Could the railwaymen move mountains?

MONT CENIS TUNNEL (1857–70)

When tunnellers, led by Germain Sommeiller, started work on the Mo Cenis tunnel they expected to progress at only 22cm a day for 20 years, b thanks to the pioneering use of new methods, the rock was moved eventua

20 times that rate and the tunnel was completed on Boxing Day of the 13th year, cutting the journey time from Paris to Turin to 18 hours.

The welfare and safety of workers was of prime concern to Sommeiller. The construction camps had family houses, schools and hospitals. At the rock face safety precautions were taken and blasting fumes were cleared by compressed air; even so 28 men died during construction.

ST GOTTHARD TUNNEL (1872–81)

The St Gotthard Tunnel was a different story altogether. The Swiss Central Railway decided to build a line from Zurich to Milan which would involve 324 bridges and over 80 tunnels including 45km which would need to spiral inside the mountains near Lucerne, and the 15km St Gotthard tunnel. They invited engineering companies to compete on price and construction period and insisted on a deposit which would be forfeited entirely if the tunnel was more than a year late.

Louis Favre, who won the contract, and others who tendered, were so inspired by the smooth and speedy progress during the latter stages of the Mont Cenis tunnel that they believed they could build the St Gotthard profitably in only 8 years, though it was longer than the Mont Cenis which had taken 13 years.

Problems started early. The construction camps at each portal took two years to build and used up an eighth of the estimated cost of the whole project. There was insufficient power to make compressed air and while rivers were diverted to provide it, workers began with hand tools, moving less than 1m of rock a day. By the time the tunnel reached the highly stressed rock further into the mountain, Favre was a worried man, behind schedule and over budget. He pressed his workers to disregard safety precautions and fed them badly, usually providing gruel and never meat.

Ground conditions proved to be much worse than Mont Cenis. The rock was so wet that dynamite became sludge and had to be put into expensive metal cases. Water poured in at an average rate of 12,000 litres a minute and had to be pumped away. Some decomposed rock turned to heavy sludge which had to be held back in places by 140cms of concrete arch.

Hundreds of men laboured side by side in water up to their knees, often knocked to the ground by outbursts of water, and assailed by flying splinters of rock squeezed by pressure from the mountain to the speed of a bullet. Visibility was drastically reduced to 20m when dust swirled after blasting, gases seeped from the rock, and heat soared above body temperature. Under pressure to work faster, tunnellers had accidents with drills, sending hot metal flying dangerously about, and became careless with rubble trucks, crashing them off the rails.

Men fearing for their health left the tunnel work after an average three month stay and, as a result, inexperienced workers replaced them. Most of the tunnellers suffered to some extent from silicosis, bronchitis, pneumonia or anaemia, even if they escaped accident. Almost 900 were so badly affected that they could never work again and 311 tunnellers died during the construction.

Before the tunnel was completed Favre himself died, probably from stress and constant exposure to the tunnel conditions. Although his family firm completed the contract, it cost them 20% more than the price they were paid

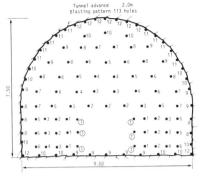

Fig. 71 *These numbers show the order in which explosives were detonated to blast a road through the Italian Dolomites. (T&T)*

BLASTING GELATINE INTRODUCED

Alfred Nobel, in whose honour Nobel prizes are awarded, invented blasting gelatine in 1875. It was first used in the St Gotthard tunnel. Nitro-cellulose (8%) is used to stabilise nitro-glycerine (92%) making it safer to use.

Fig. 72 *Liquid concrete is being pumped through specially drilled holes in a tunnel to fill gaps behind the lining. (T&T)*

Fig. 73 *Explosive charges are being placed in the mountain rock. At the bottom is the original pilot tunnel which was cut in advance of the main tunnel to check on ground conditions. (ILF Austria)*

and they were ruined. The Swiss Central Railway paid Favre's only daughter pension of £8 a month, although they had no obligation to 'do even that.

Although the St Gotthard was completed in only 9 years it had n ventilation, so passengers had to leave their hot train after the half hou journey through the tunnel and stand in the cold mountain air while thei carriages were cleaned and the windows washed.

HOOSAC TUNNEL (1851–76)

INNOVATION IN THE HOOSAC MOUNTAINS

The Crouch power drill, later adapted for the Mont Cenis was tried and abandoned in the Hoosac, as was John Wilson's first tunnelling machine; but electrical firing of explosives was successfully pioneered, and compressed air first used for American tunnelling when its engineer, Thomas Duane, invented a mechanical air compresser.

The dedication of the Favre family in completing their contract was no evident among the early contractors for the first great American mountai tunnel through the Hoosac Mountains. Originally conceived as a canal tunne it was started as a rail tunnel in 1851 only to be abandoned after 3m. Until state takeover in 1865 only 200m were built though various contractors ha worked over 9000 man days. Slow progress under state control reinforced th name tag of 'The Great Bore'. From 1869–76 a Canadian company speede up and completed the contract, but the final bill came to 17 million dollar more than the Mont Cenis for a tunnel half its length, and 15 million dolla over budget. The safety of workers hadn't caused the delays, for precautio were few. When 13 men were trapped in a shaft during a fire they suffocate because there was no emergency outlet. Nitro-glycerine was used before had been successfully mixed with a stabilising agent and with few precautio One workman was allowed to walk through the tunnel in rubber boo charging himself up from the static electricity like a battery. When he arrive at the workface he picked up the bare end of a wire and blew himself to piece

48

THE GOLDEN AGE IN THE ALPS

Greater respect for life, advances in technology and more realistic contracts characterised the golden age of Alpine rail tunnelling. The Arlberg (1880–3) opened a route from Vienna to Paris, while the 20km Simplon (1898–1906) which gave its name to the famous luxury Simplon–Orient Express, and the Loetschberg (1906–11) allowed a line to link Paris to Vienna and the East.

Work on the Simplon tunnel still claimed 96 lives as a result of the ground conditions. Water almost reached boiling point and had to be cooled by diverting an underground stream therefore creating new drainage problems and hazards. 'Spalling', in which the pressures within the mountain cause fragments of rock to break away and fly at high speed, was a constant hazard, and in places the tunnel was only prevented from being closed up by the pressure by building support walls 170cms thick.

The Loetschberg tunnel demonstrated that even expert surveys cannot always tell tunnellers what to expect. The tunnel passed under the River Kander and the survey suggested solid bedrock but warned that a silt-filled crevice might exist. In fact during the tunnelling a thin wall of rock collapsed and a million cubic feet of silt and river debris poured in and oozed quickly through the tunnel killing 25 men.

20th CENTURY HAZARDS

In this century the pioneer tunnel builders have been replaced by skilled multi-disciplinary teams, yet the hazards of nature have still lain in wait.

Surveyors mapping out the route for the Otira tunnel (1907–23) through the New Zealand Alps were often snowed up in flimsy tents. The portals had to be built in all weathers; winter snows, spring floods, and summer heat.

During the building of the Tanna tunnel through the Takiji peak in Japan over 60m of tunnel fell in suddenly, killing 16 men and trapping 17 others for days. An inflow of mud suffocated 16 other men. Water hazard was so great that a secondary tunnel had to be built to drain the main tunnel, but that became so flooded that a third tunnel was needed under the second.

Creating twin-track rail tunnels through the Appennines was also hazardous. A ball of flame roared along the ventilation tunnel of one, blew up the ventilation plant and sent hot choking fumes along the main tunnel. When water pressure caused the walls of the Great Appennine tunnel to collapse, tunnellers blocked holes in the rock with their bare hands in an attempt to save themselves from drowning, but the incident brought the death total to 97.

THE MOFFAT TUNNEL (1923–28)

In contrast progress on the 9.6km Moffat Tunnel, the first to cross the American Rockies was free of catastrophy. Only 11 men died and illness and accidents were no more common than on an average building site.

Tunnellers slept two to a room in huts which had electric light, hot showers and laundry equipment. Married men were given cottages in villages with schools and churches. Medical staff were on constant duty and strict rules banned alcohol and discouraged gambling. Workers had to wear oilskins in the tunnel and were forbidden to approach the tunnel face until it had been fully illuminated.

THE CONTRIBUTION OF ALFRED BRANDT

Alfred Brandt, chief engineer of the Simplon tunnel, invented a drill which bored into rock rather than banging it like a hammer. First tested on the Arlberg, it speeded up tunnelling on the Simplon to 5.5m a day.

Brandt's idea of constructing parallel tunnels for ventilation of the Simplon was of such vital importance that many years later it was possible to plan tunnels which could not have been built without that method. Tunnels are connectd by cross cuts and air is pushed around by fans.

THE LEWIS GIRDER

George Lewis needed a way of supporting the Moffat tunnel against almost 'fluid rock' until it could be properly lined. He devised a system of steel plates, 27m long, held in position by an extremely strong cantilevered bar, a system still used and known as the Lewis Girder. When the lining is in place the plates are used further along the tunnel.

On the Moffat tunnel, the Lewis Girder cut the excavation cost by over a third.

SHIELD METHOD FOR TANNA

The protective shield generally reserved for construction in soft ground was used on the Japanese Tanna tunnel when underground streams turned hard clay into hot flowing mud.

Fig. 74 *This Whirt TBM is on its way to creating a 5.8m bore for a mountain rail tunnel which, after lining, will be 4.7m, for the French railway system. (Spie Batignolles, France)*

MONT BLANC TUNNEL

To hold back broken rock which crumbled like rotten wood, wire netting was placed on the tunnel walls and held by giant steel pins, yet the rock in places was so hard that drills had to be fitted with tungsten caps.

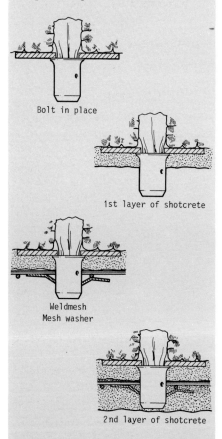

Bolt in place

1st layer of shotcrete

Weldmesh
Mesh washer

2nd layer of shotcrete

Fig. 75 *Wire mesh between two layers of shotcrete, held in place by special washers, was used to line the Swiss Sengg alpine road tunnel. (T&T)*

The tunnel resulted from an interesting politica! deal between a Denve railroad company and the City of Denver, in which the pilot tunnel was use for ventilation during construction of the main railway tunnel, and was the converted to supply water to the city. Excavating the tunnels in parallel n only helped in ventilating the work but allowed the blasting cycles to be co ordinated keeping the tunnellers fully employed at all times.

Three quarters of a million tons of the Rockies were removed durin construction, but for travellers it was worth it: the 12 minute tunnel journe reduced considerably the 7 hour trip from Denver to Salt Lake City.

ROAD TUNNELS THROUGH THE MOUNTAINS

Since the 1950s the popularity of the motor car and heavy goods vehicle ha led to a world wide expansion in the number of mountain road tunnels.

In 1962, the Great St Bernard tunnel provided a link between Italy an Switzerland, replacing a road which was passable for no more than thre months a year and even then only by light vehicles. The 11.6km Mont Blar tunnel linked the motorways of France and Italy. These tunnels were mor sophisticated than the rail ones, needing to cope with noxious exhaust fume and provide adequate safety arrangements for the drivers of the hundreds o individual vehicles using the tunnels at any one time.

The Mont Blanc tunnel has served a million drivers a year since it wa opened. In 1990, when other Italian road construction is completed, drive will be able to travel through it and other motorway tunnels from Calais t Trieste on the Yugoslav border without so much as a traffic light to interru their journey and, incidentally, without seeing much of France or Italy eithe

Fig. 76 *Portal of the Seelisberg road tunnel through the Alps which linked Italy and Germany in 1978. (Marti Inter, Switzerland)*

Fig. 77 *A drilling rig at work inside a Norwegian mountain. (Atlas Copco, Sweden)*

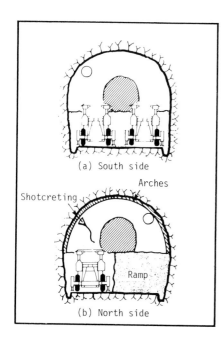

(a) South side

Arches

Shotcreting

Ramp

(b) North side

Fig. 78 *New machine-mounted high frequency drills were used in 1983 to create a motorway tunnel through the Austrian Alps by enlarging the pilot tunnel. On one side two machines were able to drill together, but from the other only a half of the tunnel could be drilled at a time. (T&T)*

Fig. 79 *Portal of the Dullin alpine road tunnel near Lyon in France. (Spi Batignolles, France)*

Fig. 80 *Creating a cavern in the mountain. The top heading was dug first, wor continues in the lower half. (Nitro Nobel AB Sweden)*

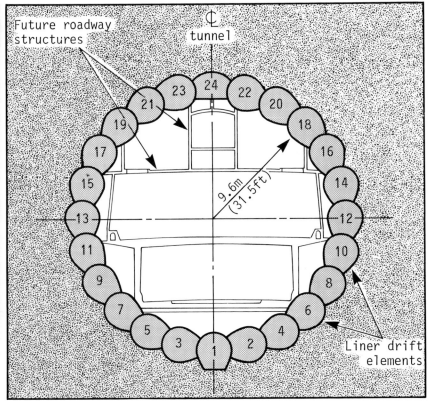

Future roadway structures

Ͼ tunnel

9.6m (31.5ft)

Liner drift elements

Fig. 81 *To create a road tunnel with a 25m diameter in Washington Seattle USA, twenty four drifts were bored around the perimeter of the unstable ground and filled in to support the tunnel. This technique is known as the multiple drift method. (T&T)*

A mere decade after the opening of the two tunnels traffic demand was so great that a third, the Gotthard Road Tunnel, was built to provide a link 16.3km long between northern and southern Europe. The Arlberg Expressway tunnel linked Paris with Eastern Europe. The Arlberg has an enclosed tube resting on a bridge in the middle of it where it passes over a gorge. This protects drivers from the weather and the confusion of a transfer from tunnel to bridge and back – but denies them the view.

So ordinary has much mountain tunnel construction now become that an inclined shaft 1730m long has been dug through the Pitztaler glacier in the Austrian Tyrol 3693m above sea level just to carry a pair of rail-mounted passenger cars for skiers in the Pitz valley. Among projects to develop a network of European high speed trains is a 40km rail tunnel linking Italy and Switzerland.

Ambitious mountain projects are being considered and constructed all over the world nowadays, so perhaps it is just as well to illustrate the continuing power of nature with a story from the USA.

EISENHOWER MEMORIAL TUNNEL (1967–79)

The Eisenhower Memorial tunnel was designed as a two lane road tunnel 17m wide and 20m high, to be fitted with all the latest equipment. Because it had to pass through the relatively soft rock of the Loveland Fault in the Rockies west of Denver, a boring machine protected by a shield was chosen for the work. But the Rockies just wouldn't yield and squeezed in on the tunnel stopping work for two years, forcing the use of multiple headings, and doubling the cost to a hundred million dollars.

THE NEW AUSTRIAN TUNNELLING METHOD (NATM)

NATM's name derives from early in the 19th Century when the Belgians, Germans, English, Italians and Austrians developed different national methods of tunnel excavation. This new technique is a variation of the Austrian method.

It is based on the theory that pressures in the rock will allow a natural arch to form for most of the length of a tunnel carved out of hard rock. The initial support is designed to encourage this natural arch, whereas in other methods walls and the arch are supported firmly and expensively at an early stage. NATM allows observation of the areas where the ground squeezes in and these are then heavily reinforced, while only a thin lining is placed elsewhere. Indeed some tunnels are left unlined.

Fig. 82 *Marc Isambard Brunel's tunnelling shield, the first of many shields used to protect tunnellers in soft wet ground, in use during construction of the Thames tunnel. (Science Photo Library UK)*

8
TUNNELLING UNDERWATER

Over 4000 years ago slaves dug a great trench into the mud of the Euphrate during the dry season and built a tunnel which allowed a passage under th mighty river when it was once more in full flow.

The next great river tunnel was under London's Thames. Richar Trevithick began work in 1807 but his tunnel was flooded and the project wa abandoned in 1808.

THAMES TUNNEL 1825–43

In 1824 Marc Isambard Brunel formed his Thames Tunnel Company wit the Duke of Wellington among his subscribers, and the following March having moved house to be near the work, he laid the first brick at Rotherhith His son Isambard Kingdom Brunel, then only 18, laid the second.

The father and son team courted much publicity for their venture Isambard, having been appointed Chief Engineer at the age of 20, held h 21st birthday party in the tunnel workings, and 700 people attended a conce

Fig. 83 *The top of the Rotherhithe shaft of the Brunels' Thames tunnel which now houses a museum. (T&T)*

Fig. 84 *Precast concrete road deck units are being placed in position in 1967 in the Blackwall tunnel in England. (Balfour Beatty UK)*

TUNNELLING SHIELDS

Marc Isambard Brunel's shield, patented in 1818 and used on the Thames tunnel, allowed tunnels to be dug in soft wet ground for the first time. It was designed in a curious way. Brunel never went anywhere without a magnifying glass, and one day, supervising work on a tunnel in Chatham dockyard, he noticed ship-worms destroying timber. He studied the worms as they ate the wood and excreted it to form a smooth lining to the holes they had created. Brunel copied their action by creating an iron cylinder from inside which men could cut away the ground. They were followed by others who lined the walls with bricks.

Greathead Shield

In 1869, Barlow and Greathead, working on another Thames crossing, and Beach, tunnelling in New York, independently devised a shield, the front end of which could be partly or wholly closed to prevent inflow of soft ground. Often used in compressed air, the Greathead shield is still the basis of much tunnelling.

Bentonite Shield

In the 1960s a British engineer, John Bartlett invented a shield incorporating the use of a bentonite slurry which allows tunnelling without the use of compressed air. It has since been developed, mainly in Japan and Germany, for robot machines to excavate and line tunnels of all kinds.

of classical music there. But days afterwards the river flooded in and Isambard became a hero when he saved the lives of some of his fellow tunnellers. A second flood was serious enough to put Isambard into hospital and end work for 7 years. A giant mirror was placed at the end of the workings and visitors paid to enter the tunnel and look at themselves inside it.

By the time the tunnel was completed Isambard was renowned as a great engineer. When it opened, more than 50,000 people paid a toll to walk through it, but it never became a successful route for horse-drawn traffic and was losing money when taken over by the railways in 1860. There is now a Brunel exhibition centre at the Rotherhithe entrance.

MORE THAMES TUNNELS

The building of a Thames railway tunnel in 1869 led to the development of the Greathead shield. The Blackwall tunnel (1892–97) was notable because no lives were lost and only three cases of permanent injury recorded during its construction in compressed air. Compressed air was also used during the building of the 1904–8 Rotherhithe tunnel.

The 1963 Dartford road tunnel and the 1968 Blackwall tunnel under the Thames were part of the 1960s motorway building projects which included tunnels under the Clyde in 1963 and Tyne in 1967.

Fig. 85 *Tunnellers digging a shaft in the bed of the River Tyne, UK in air compressed to match the pressure of the river, thus making sure that water will not push its way into the shaft as the men dig it. The shaft was later filled with concrete to help support the Redlaugh Bridge. (Edmund Nuttall UK)*

IMMERSED TUBES

Tunnelling under waterways using shields and compressed air is expensive and can be dangerous, so for many crossings prefabricated tubes are now lowered into a trench on the river bed and connected.

The American System

This system was first used in America between 1906 and 1910, when 62m lengths of steel tube encased in concrete were linked under the Detroit river to create a railway tunnel.

Since 1928, when the first was built in Oakland, California, many

UNDER THE SEVERN

The Severn estuary, which experiences the highest tides in Europe, was a barrier to transport between South West England and the rest of Britain. In 1873 the Great Western Railway Company began work on 7km of double track railway. Half was to be under the river, a mammoth task needing 36,79- tons of cement, over 76 million bricks and 4000 people working at the same time.

The main problem was water. In the words of its engineer, Thomas Walker, 'The water pumped from the Severn Tunnel during the time of it construction would form a lake 3 miles square and 10 yards deep.' After an underground flow known as 'The Big Spring' broke into the tunnel, for more than a year an average of 24 million gallons of water a day had to be pumped out, as much as 30 million on some days.

Improvisation by tunnellers was common in those days and once, when the tunnel began to leak under a part of the river which was only 1m deep, Walker ordered the men to link hands and wade out. The position of the hole was discovered when one of them fell into it.

Even after additional pumps had been installed to cope with 'the Big Spring', a tidal wave up the channel resulted in the tunnel being flooded gain. Once more it was pumped out, and was finished in 1886. In 1890 ten oal trains from South Wales moved 3000 tons of coal through the tunnel in 2 hours to fuel the Fleet at Portsmouth. Up to 150 trains a day can still use the unnel and, if properly maintained, it will last for another 100 years.

In the early 1970s an electric cable tunnel was built under the estuaries of he Severn and Wye rivers.

MERSEY TUNNELS

A hundred years ago Liverpool was a thriving and expanding port, serving orthwest England, but it needed a rail link under the Mersey to Birkenhead nd the south. Beaumont's power drill was used to tunnel from the irkenhead end and achieved a rate of 10m a day. But because the ground as so unstable the drill had to be stopped regularly and overall progress was o faster than the blasting cycle from the Liverpool end, an operation so noisy hat the Admiral of the Grand Fleet anchored above thought his ships were eing attacked and called a full war alert.

Road tunnels were completed under the Mersey in 1934, 1953 and 1971.

RAIL TUNNELS AROUND THE WORLD

At the turn of the 19th century, railway companies around the world ommissioned tunnels to shorten journeys wherever rivers got in their way. or instance, in 1890 the Sarnia tunnel under the St Clair river built for the Canadian Grand Trunk Railway linked Ontario to Michigan in the USA.

TUNNELS UNDER THE HUDSON

n the 1870s a miner and Western railroad builder called Dewitt Clinton Haskin arrived in New York with plans to tunnel under the Hudson river. He proclaimed that his tunnel could be built in 3 years without the great expense of a shield and using only compressed air to support the ground. The tunnel vould be illuminated by gas jets and would allow steam trains to reach Manhattan from New Jersey.

Fifteen years later and after seven false starts, which had cost Haskin and is backers most of their 10 million dollars, work was resumed using a shield. Even then the ground was so wet that the mud had to be baked by kerosene amps before it could be tunnelled. When the tunnel was completed in 1909 Haskin had quietly disappeared.

By the 1920s there were so many cars in New York that a tunnel under the Hudson was needed for them. It was more than 2.5km long and they filled the ir with noxious fumes as they passed through. Chief Engineer Clifford M Holland devised a special ventilation system which forced 400,000 cubic metres of air a minute into the tunnel. He became so involved in his work that e ate and often slept in the tunnel, making himself ill in the process. He died efore this, the world's first long vehicle tunnel, was completed in 1927. Its ame was changed to the Holland tunnel in his honour. Within a short time it vas being used by 13 million cars a year.

Two-lane road tunnels under the Hudson to link New Jersey with Manhatten were completed in 1937, 1945 and 1957. Each is over 2km long. All were shield driven in compressed air and have cast-iron linings.

immersed tube road tunnels have been created in the USA, notably in Virginia, Detroit, Baltimore and across Chesapeake Bay.

The European Version

A European variation which involves a rectangular shaped tube was developed by Christiani and Neilsen in 1936 for a Rotterdam river crossing. A uniform base is created for this system by injecting sand between the bottom of the trench and the underside of the tunnel.

Underwater Motorways

Using this method the 48m wide J. F. Kennedy tunnel in Antwerp, Belgium, carries 6 road lanes, 2 railway tracks and a pedestrian and cycle duct. The slightly wider Doordrecht tunnel in Holland carries 8 traffic lanes.

VERTICAL TRANSVERSE FLOW VENTILATION

Clifford Holland's ventilation system for his tunnel under the Hudson involved fresh air being pumped in at kerb level. This rose, mixed with the exhaust fumes and was sucked out by fans in the roof. Fresh air was thus supplied without gusts of wind being blown through the tunnel. This system has been used on many other road tunnels.

Fig. 86 *The Seikan tunnel.*
(P. Middleton UK)

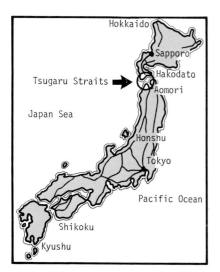

Fig. 87 *Location of Japan's Seikan tunnel. (T&T)*

TUNNELS OF JAPAN

The Japanese have built more transport tunnels than any other nation since their first railway tunnel in 1874. Their underwater tunnels include the Kanmon rail tunnel (1942) and road tunnel (1958). The Shinkannon rail tunnel, completed in 1975, involved almost 3km of underwater construction.

THE SEIKAN TUNNEL

The biggest challenge to Japanese tunnellers was the Seikan rail tunnel, 23.3km of its 53.9km being under the sea and passing through unstable ground in an earthquake zone.

Ferry Accident

Geological investigations for the Seikan to link the islands of Honshu and Hokkaida under the Tsugaru Strait began in 1946, but it was not until the death of 1430 people in a ferry boat accident during a typhoon in September 1954, that detailed planning was undertaken.

Excavation began in 1964, but the tunnel was not bored through until 1985. It is to come into service in 1988. Progress was slow because much of the ground had first to be strengthened by grouting.

Flooding

Despite precautions the tunnel was flooded in 1970, twice in 1974, and again in 1976. During these incidents a total of 3700 cubic metres of earth and sand were deposited in it. The most serious flood engulfed 3km of the service tunnel and 1.5km of the rail tunnel.

The tunnel was intended to reduce rail travel time from Tokyo to Sapporo, the main city of Hokkaido, from 14 to less than 6 hours. But during its construction an air service has been developed which takes only 85 minutes.

Profitability Doubts

In the late 1980s doubts have been expressed about the profitability of a rail link through a tunnel which has cost 10 times its budget. Serious consideration was given to using it for oil storage or even mushroom cultivation.

UNDERWATER TUNNELS TODAY

All over the world great waterways are being crossed quickly, safely and easily through tunnels. Among the busiest are the Maas in Rotterdam and the Lincoln and Holland in New York.

Hong Kong Harbour

In the 10 years following its completion in 1972, 250 million vehicle journeys were made through the Hong Kong Cross-Harbour tunnel linking Hong Kong with mainland Kowloon, as many as 35,000 a day. Even so, the 8.5km immersed tube tunnel wasn't sufficient for the demand, nor was the rail tunnel opened in 1981. Now a third tunnel carrying both road and rail traffic is to be built.

Tokyo Bay, Japan

In Japan, 30,000 cars a day will soon be able to cross Tokyo Bay using a 14.5km bridge and tunnel system being built to withstand typhoons and earthquakes. It will cut 75 minutes each way off journey times.

A Tunnel for Industry

Not all underwater tunnels are built to serve demand, some are designed to create it, such as the one planned under the Ems river to provide a motorway link to Eastern Friesland in Germany and encourage industrial development of the area.

Elbe Tunnel Modernisation

Old tunnels aren't always left to rot when more sophisticated ones are needed. The 1908 Elbe tunnel under Hamburg's river was designed for horse drawn carriages which had to be lowered into it by lift. Between 1981 and 1983 it was completely modernised by tunnellers working from a compressed air chamber on the river bed.

Fig. 88 *Proposed route of an immersed tube under Sydney harbour. The famous bridge is on the right. (T&T)*

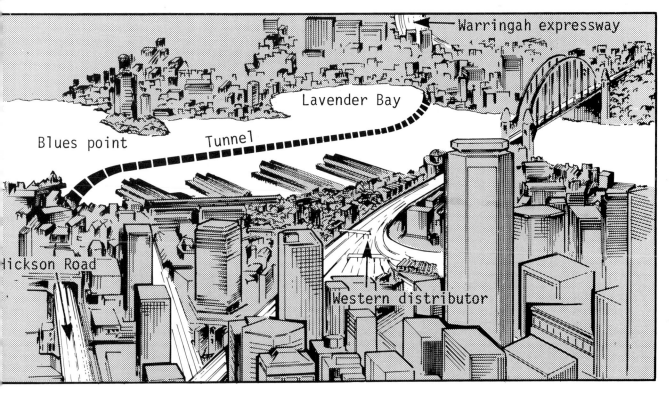

Fig. 89   *Old Haymarket entrance to the First Mersey road tunnel.*

Fig. 90   *Tunnellers at work under the Mersey in 1930.*

Fig. 91 *Man using a spade to help create a ventilation station for the Mersey tunnel in 1932. Even today many tunnellers work with hand tools on small construction jobs because the use of sophisticated machinery is uneconomic.*

Fig. 92 *When work stopped for the weekend in 1928, this part of the construction under the Mersey was temporarily boarded up. This is still common practice, but when the ground is soft no gaps can be left and timbers fit neatly together.*

Fig. 93 *Tunnellers at work in 1928. Nowadays special clothing and head gear are worn and smoking is forbidden.*

Fig. 94 *The First Mersey road tunnel in 1934.*

Fig. 95 a&b   *Assembled machinery (Left) and the mole, as the tunnel boring machine was known, (Right) enter the Second M*
road tunnel.

Fig. 96   *The mole breaks through.*

Fig. 97   *Celebrating the mole break-though in the Second Mersey road tunnel. Martin Knights, co-author of this book can be seen on the top deck, fifth from the left.*

Fig. 98   *Her Majesty Queen Eliza-*
beth II drives through the tunnel.

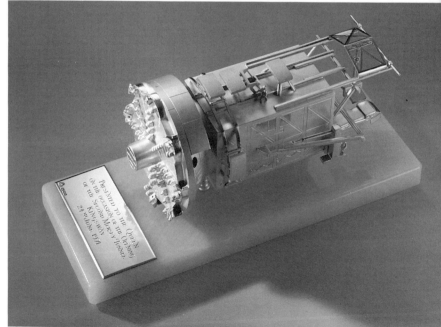

Fig. 99   *A model of the mole presented*
to Her Majesty on June 24th 1971 to
commemorate the tunnel opening.
(All photographs of Mersey Tunnel
Edmund Nuttall UK)

9
THE CHANNEL TUNNEL

Fig. 100 *A diamond drill boring machine of the kind used to sink the shafts for the Channel tunnel in 1875. (Science Photo Library UK)*

is only 6000 years since the sea made an island of what is now Britain. The ritish have grown proud of their independent island heritage, while the rench, sharing land borders with other countries, have no strong feelings bout one with England.

The decision to join the European Economic Community seemed to many f the British to herald the end of their independence; for them, being ttached to the land mass of Europe by a tunnel was the final indignity.

It is against the background of these emotions that the long history of the hannel tunnel can be understood, for it has been technically possible for a entury or more.

The possibility of a tunnel was first mooted in 1802 when Albert Mathieu isplayed plans in Paris for a tunnel which would be illuminated by oil lamps nd ventilated by chimneys projecting above the sea into the open air. Horses ould pull coachloads of passengers through it, with an artificial island in the niddle of the Channel to provide for changes of horses. At the Peace of miens Napoleon Bonaparte and Charles James Fox discussed the scheme as potential joint project.

In 1834 Aimé Thome de Gamond, a man passionately devoted to the stablishment of a Channel crossing, proposed submerging an iron tube. etween 1835 and 1836 he suggested five types of bridge, then in 1842 again urned his mind to a tunnel.

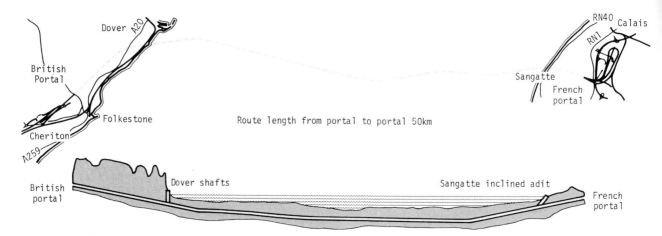

Fig. 101 *The route of the Channel tunnel. (T&T)*

In 1855, at the age of 48, he dived to the bottom of the Channel, taking on two precautions. He wore pads of buttered lint on his ears to protect the from the water pressure, and put a spoonful of olive oil into his mouth so th he could expel air from his lungs without allowing water at high pressure force its way in. He carried heavy bags of flint to act as ballast and dived ove 30m to collect geological specimens from the Channel bed. Around his wai he wore a belt of inflated pigs' bladders which could be used to haul hi quickly to the surface. During one descent he was attacked by huge cong eels which seized his arms and legs and bit him on the chin.

His tunnel was to have 12 artificial islands, topped by lighthouses, fro which ventilation shafts would be sunk. The shafts were designed with s valves so that in the event of war, either Britain or France could flood tl tunnel. De Gamond also planned to build an international port on the Varn a submerged shelf only 5m underwater in places, about 10 miles o Folkestone.

In the Spring of 1856, Napoleon III expressed an interest in the schen and British engineers Stephenson, Brunel and Joseph Locke promised collaborate. Queen Victoria, who suffered from sea-sickness, said, 'You ma tell the French engineer that if he can accomplish it, I will give him my blessir in my own name and in the name of all the ladies of England.'

But two years later an attempt to assassinate Napoleon III alleged employed bombs made in Birmingham – and talk of a tunnel ceased. By 18' de Gamond, having spent 35 years and a small fortune promoting a cros

Fig. 102 *An electrically driven Whitaker boring machine of this type began work in 1930. But the UK parliament voted 51% to 49% against the tunnel. The machine was later found abandoned in a field in Kent. (T&T)*

Channel link, was living in humble circumstances, supported by his daughter who gave piano lessons.

The successful building of the Alpine tunnels had given railroad owners and tunnellers confidence, and William Low, an engineer with a Welsh mining background, proposed two single track railway tunnels linked by cross cuts for ventilation, the basis of today's Channel Tunnel plans.

Low was involved in one of three English tunnel consortia in the 1870s, but it was a rival group, headed by Sir Edward Watkin, which won support. The son of a Lancashire cotton merchant and chairman of three railway companies, he saw the benefits of a railway line linking Manchester to the continent, and called upon the services of Colonel Frederick Beaumont, an engineer who had tried out a compressed-air boring machine under the Mersey, where it had performed well. They anticipated cutting through the chalk under the Channel at the rate of 15m a day.

Compressed air would also ventilate the tunnel. A new invention, electric light, would illuminate it. Despite many objections, enabling legislation was passed and work was started.

To promote the tunnel, guests were lowered 50m in large buckets to inspect the machinery, then enjoyed either a champagne party in the tunnel or a champagne lunch in Dover.

All to no avail. Despite the lavish entertainment and the lobbying of influential people, Sir Garnet Wolseley, who claimed that the tunnel offered an easy invasion route and was a serious threat to the security of the nation, led

Fig. 103 *Contractors using the 1973 central tunnel to marshal equipment for the 1980s project. The tunnel is for access to the cliff top. (Eurotunnel UK/France)*

Fig. 104 *Model of the Priestley boring machine which began work on the Channel tunnel in 1973. (Edmund Nuttall UK)*

Fig. 105 *The TBM makes its way down an open cut adit to the 1973 start of the Channel tunnel. (Edmund Nuttall UK)*

Fig. 106 *Unwanted tunnel lining segments in stock at the Ashford casting yard in October 1974 after cancellation of the tunnel. (Edmund Nuttall UK)*

a strong protest movement. Amid a furious clamour in parliament and the press, work was stopped. In 1888 Sir Edward Watkin tried for the last time to win a vote in parliament and failed.

The signing of the Entente Cordiale in 1904 started another round of proposals, which were defeated in 1907 and 1914. Later, it was considered that a tunnel supply route to France during World War I could have brought victory by 1916.

In 1924 and 1930 the Committee of Imperial Defence stifled initiatives again, and after the Second World War it was stated that the Germans had considered tunnelling from France to invade England.

British Railways promoted the idea of a tunnel, and in 1955 Harold Macmillan the Minister of Defence said that there were scarcely any military objections.

His statement encouraged new interest and in July 1957 a Channel Tunnel Study Group was formed. By 1963 samples taken from under the Channel indicated the presence of a layer of chalk which would be ideal for tunnelling.

Work actually began on a railway tunnel in 1973, but with a change of political control in Britain in 1974, the project was stopped.

In 1979 British Rail published new plans for a rail tunnel, but Margaret Thatcher's Conservative government decided to invite proposals for a link which would be financed privately, and built not by political decision but on its merits as a commercially viable enterprise.

Examination of British trade and passenger traffic on the cross-Channel ferries suggested that a link would soon be necessary to prevent overcrowding of the already busy Channel sea lanes. A tunnel should be built and could be operated at a profit.

Proposals put forward by consortia of construction companies and other institutions included suspension and cable bridges, a tunnel between London and Paris and two proposals which involved tunnelling between Folkestone and Calais. The consortia would be required to raise the hundreds of millions of pounds necessary to build the links, and offer shares to the public.

A proposal by Euroroute involved the creation of two artificial islands near the coast which cars would reach by bridge. Motorists would then drive down spirals and share a submerged tube with a twin track railway line.

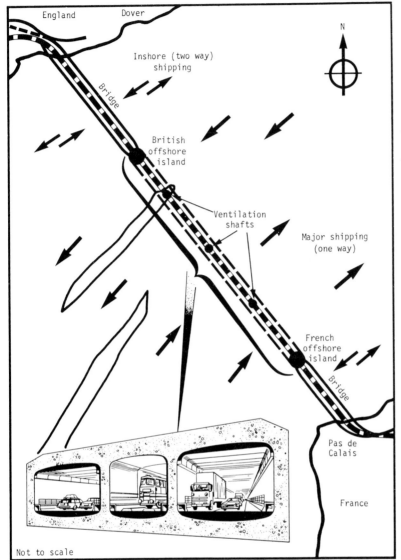

Not to scale

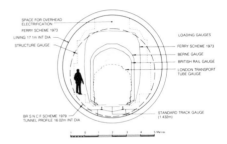

Fig. 107 *The immersed tube and bridge proposal for crossing the English channel which was rejected in 1986. (T&T)*

Fig. 108 *Sizes of trains and shuttles which will use the Channel tunnel compared to ordinary rail and metro trains. (T&T)*

The proposal selected in January 1986 by the British and French governments was the one put forward by the Channel Tunnel Group and France Manche, later called Euro-Tunnel. It was for two 7.6m diameter tunnels linked by cross passages every 375m to a 4.8m diameter service tunnel, all to be bored beneath the sea bed for 37.5km of the 49.2km route between Cheriton near Folkestone and Sangatte near Calais.

The main tunnels are designed for giant shuttle trains which will carry cars, coaches and lorries through the tunnel in about 30 minutes. The capacity of the link is for 24 shuttles an hour in each direction, with one leaving every 2½ minutes. However, a service every 10 to 30 minutes depending on the time of day running for 24 hours every day of the year, is planned initially.

Drivers arriving by flyover from the M20 in England will pay at a toll booth and pass through British and French customs and immigration. Refreshments and duty free shopping will be available. The loading system, modelled on one used by Swiss Alpine railways, will cater for 4000 vehicles an hour.

Fig. 109 *A train in the Channel tunnel. This and similar illustrations are artists impressions of how things will be. (Eurotunnel UK/France)*

EXCAVATING THE TUNNEL

The tunnel will be excavated from each side of the Channel by a total of 11 tunnel boring machines, and lined with either cast iron or pre-cast conrete sections depending on ground conditions. Work will be continuous, 24 hours a day, 7 days a week. On the French side the ground will need to be grouted and a shield used until the chalk layer is reached.

Almost 5 million cubic metres of spoil from the British side will be carried out by 200 muck cars. It will be used to level the terminal site and reclaim land for the tunnel access and recreational use near the entrance. Up to 4.5 million cubic metres from the French side will be disposed of south of Sangatte.

Fig. 110   *Drive-through customs clearance for the Channel tunnel. (Eurotunnel UK/France)*

Fig. 111   *Driving onto the Channel tunnel shuttle. (Eurotunnel UK/France)*

SHUTTLE TRAINS

The tourist shuttles to be pulled by electric locomotives through the Channel tunnel will be the biggest passenger trains ever built, over 1m higher and 1.5m wider than normal trains.

Each one will have 26 carriages, half double deckers for cars, half single deckers for coaches and tall vehicles. To allow coaches to drive in, openings on the end wagons will need to be 16m long on each side.

So that vehicles can drive straight through the shuttle, each carriage will have openings more than 3m wide which will be closed off by shutters during the journey.

Wagons on the freight shuttle will carry one vehicle each.

TUNNEL SAFETY

The risk of accidents will be minimised by not allowing cars to be driven through the tunnel.

Control systems and standby locomotives will reduce dangers.

Each wagon will carry either one goods vehicle, or up to ten cars, or a coach and a car, and will have emergency exits for evacuating passengers, and fire and smoke resistant shutters, so that any fire which breaks out can be contained within the wagon in transit. If the fire persists, the wagon can be disconnected from the rest of the shuttle.

The service tunnel is designed to be used as a safe haven and escape route in any larger scale incident.

The tunnels are set in solid rock too far below the sea bed for an accident or an attack to flood the tunnel.

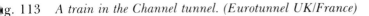

Fig. 112   Shuttle/rail tunnels and the central service tunnel which together make up the Channel tunnel. (Eurotunnel UK/France)

Fig. 113   A train in the Channel tunnel. (Eurotunnel UK/France)

VENTILATION

Ventilation designers have to assume that 2000 people will be in the tunnel at any time and arrange for air to be available to them, both on a normal journey and in the event of a breakdown.

A major problem is the effect of fast trains on the flow and temperature of the air. When trains move at high speed in a confined space they create tremendous air pressure around them. This is called the piston effect and a system of ducts will be used to cope with it.

Drivers from France will use Autoroute 26 which is linked by motorway t
Paris and the south, Rheims and the south east, Brussels and Germany, Ghen
and Amsterdam. They will pass through a terminal to the South West o
Calais.

During the journey drivers will be able to take a rest, listen to their radio
through a tunnel frequency, or walk around the shuttle using vendin
machines and toilets or watch information videos. On arrival, it will b
possible to drive off without further formalities.

Customs clearance of freight will take place at a special depot at Ashford i
Kent for road traffic and at the Willesden depot in London for rail traffi

Special passenger trains, able to run on the British and French rail system
will be 'Customs cleared' at Waterloo in London, Ashford in Kent, Paris an
Brussels. Journey times from London are scheduled to be 3hrs 15mins t
Paris, 2hrs 55mins to Brussels.

These services are expected to come into operation early in 1993 when it
anticipated that the tunnel will cater for 20 million passengers a year, makin
it about half as busy as the most popular stretches of the M1 motorway. It
predicted that there will still be sufficient demand for ferry services for the
to continue.

Before then, though, the tunnel has to be built.

The major problems for tunnellers from France are the unstable nature o
the ground before they reach the chalk layer and possible effect on the wate
table during construction of the terminal. This could, unless special measure
are taken, result in salt water seeping into the fresh water table beneath th
land mass. Despite a number of environmental problems, the proposals hav
been generally welcomed in France as an opportunity to create employmer
in a relatively underdeveloped area.

In England apart from worries about the loss of island identity, qualm
about rabies, and disquiet among those who earn their livelihood from fer
traffic, the main concerns have been about the effect of the tunnel on life i
Kent, and on regional development.

Because of increases in traffic, the development it may attract and th
location of the terminal in a designated Area of Outstanding Natural Beaut
many people in Kent consider that their lifestyle will suffer, even though th
buildings associated with the tunnel will eventually be landscaped. On th
other hand freight trains may replace as many as 1500 large lorries.

The concern of the British regions is that the tunnel will create yet mor
centralisation of investment and trade in the South East, a worry reinforce
by the siting of the rail terminals and road freight depot. However, British ra
plan to run services for freight and passengers from regional sites.

When Britain becomes part of the mainland of Europe, though, the por
along the west coast of Scotland, Wales and England will become the Englisl
speaking gateway to the business and tourist attractions of Europe for tran
Atlantic shipping, which will no longer have to sail further east for a mainlan
harbour, saving up to one and a half days.

With sufficient initiative and demand, regional Customs clearance centre
for road and rail freight can be opened, and direct passenger trains schedule
from cities other than London, using either on-train Customs clearance o
terminals.

The Channel Tunnel offers a new dimension to the British people
become citizens of mainland Europe.

10 TUNNELS OF THE FUTURE

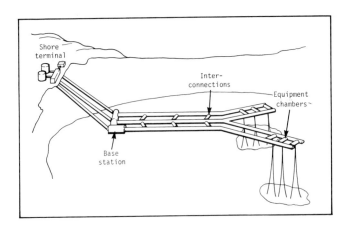

Fig. 114 *To avoid fishing grounds close to the shore, Norwegian oil from the Troll field may be brought ashore by drilling from undersea platforms arranged like this. (T&T)*

any tunnels of the future will take their shape from today's research and evelopment.

In mining, for instance, the Robbins Company of America are testing Mobile Miners' with cutting arms which can reach in all directions and cut rough the hardest of rock without blasting.

unnels for Cities

In older cities many service tunnels need replacing, and for the rapidly xpanding populations of the Third World, water and sewage tunnels are the nly alternative to famine and disease. Japanese-built remote controlled obots, directed by lasers which can go around corners and avoid the expense sinking shafts below busy city streets, are ideal for creating such tunnels.

unnels Already Planned

Some vast schemes have already been planned for the next 20 years, such as 50km water supply tunnel for California, and the 200km of tunnels needed release the untapped hydro-electric capacity of India by building power ations in the Himalayas.

he Search for Power

Other power schemes are more speculative, such as Sweden's investigation shafts to search for methane gas deep within the Earth, and Norwegian ans to develop the Troll oilfield, 55km off the coast, from shafts sunk on nd and tunnels reaching under the sea.

Some tunnels which have been talked about for a long time may be built at

Fig. 115 *In the 1970s shafts were sunk to a depth of over 1000m in the Grant's Mineral Belt of New Mexico. As a result of that achievement, tunnellers in the USA are considering sinking shafts onshore to below the level of the ocean bed then tunnelling out to offshore oil. (T&T)*

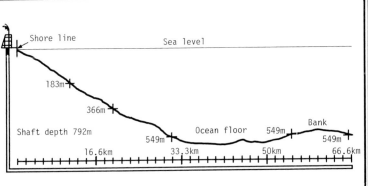

g 115i (Left) *How the tunnels would be positioned nder the ocean.*

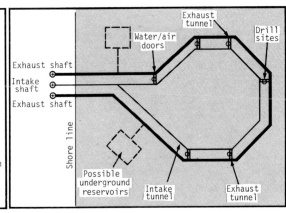

Fig 115ii (Right) *The layout of the drilling system under the ocean.*

last. One is the link between Africa and Europe across the Straits of Gibralta first considered in 1908. Another is a tunnel planned between Italy and Sicil

Not all the tunnels mooted get built. In 1879 it was proposed to remove I million cubic metres of soil along a tunnel route to link the Atlantic and Pacif oceans, but the scheme died when the Panama canal opened.

New Technology

New technology may be used to make dreams come true. Denmark has or peninsula and 483 islands. So far it has not been economically viable consider either linking them or to creating tunnels to Denmark or Swede Norway has the same problem with fjords. Now consideration is being give to the cheaper method of using immersed tubes which would not be placed c the bed, but would float below shipping levels, anchored to the bed whic might be many metres deeper.

Moon Caverns

The development of caverns for food and fuel storage, and even hot wat for heating, is likely to expand; cities built completely underground are technical possibility. Certainly a moon colony is as likely to be create underground as on the surface.

In the meantime, if cities continue to grow as they have during this centur underground shopping malls such as those in Canada and Japan, spor facilities and underground railway systems will all become more common

Future of Cities

It is dangerous, however, to assume the direction which progress will tak Our potential to communicate with each other electronically and the dislil which many people have of commuting to large, impersonal, crime-ridde cities could lead to a new system of living in smaller communities and workir from home; offices would then stand empty and metros be unused. Wh would that mean for tunnellers?

Technological Leaps Forward

Fast developing technology is contributing to major leaps forward tunnelling, not least of which are remote control and robotries in dangero situations, thus promoting safety.

If it proves possible to devise a tunnel which is airless and frictionless ar can be insulated from the heat of the rock within the earth, then the dream mathematician Paul Cooper could become reality – a 42 minute journey fro any city on Earth to any other. A vehicle would be dropped into a tunn where it would accelerate and gather enough kinetic energy to emerge at tl other end against the force of gravity in exactly 42.2 minutes whatever tl distance.

For the building of most tunnels, however, the force to be overcome will l that of human inertia. The will to build and the funds to carry out a proje must exist together; until they do, even the simplest projects cannot get off tl ground. The Channel Tunnel is certainly a case in point. By ensuring that tl tunnel can be a profitable railway enterprise the public are being encourage to invest and share in the future profits. Who knows, a road tunnel may soc follow.

11
TUNNEL BUILDERS OF TODAY AND TOMORROW

This chapter has two purposes, the first is to describe the sort of people who are involved in building tunnels; the second to show the knowledge and skills you would need to become a tunnel builder yourself.

Regardless of paper qualifications it is still true that the geologists who understand the nature of the ground best are the ones who have seen most rocks, and that the best tunnellers are the ones who have driven most tunnels. Just as no two rocks are exactly alike, no two tunnels are the same. Experience forms the basis of a tunneller's expertise.

Fig. 116 *These men are inspecting a shaft built in the Mersey estuary, UK as part of a scheme to reduce pollution. The precast concrete segments are the largest ever produced. Each weighs 7 tons. The shaft is 24m deep and is waterproofed by pre-formed rubber gaskets. (Buchan UK)*

Decision Making

Tunnels are built for a purpose and for a client. The client may be a publ[ic] institution, such as a municipal water authority, or a business, such as [a] railway, a mine or the owners of a toll road.

Often clients have options to consider which do not involve tunnels. If [a] mountain stands between two cities they may route the road to join the[m] round the side of the mountain rather than tunnel through it. If they need t[o] cross a river they can choose between a tunnel, a bridge, a ferry, even a lig[ht] plane or helicopter service. Management, economic planning and co[st] accountancy skills to assess all the options and take account of political a[nd] environmental issues affecting their choice are needed. Planners usual[ly] estimate the costs of the options by using a sophisticated computer progra[m].

Science in Tunnelling

Tunnels have to be planned, often years before building begins. Enginee[rs] and surveyors inspect the route and geologists report on ground conditio[ns]. Both use sophisticated electronic measuring equipment and compute[r] analysis of their observations and rock samples. They need a knowledge [of] mathematics, mechanics and statistical analysis. Experts who examine th[e] rock samples need to know physics as well, to help in their prediction of wh[at] will happen when the ground is tunnelled. This knowledge is applied [by] ground treatment and equipment specialists so the way the ground will b[e] excavated can be decided.

Designing and Costing the Tunnel

Once the route and construction method have been established the rest [of] the tunnel can be designed and costed in principle. All this preparation [is] carried out by a team led by a Civil or Mining Engineer with a speciali[st] understanding of tunnelling.

Engineers in Tunnels

In the construction of a tunnel, engineers will be employed by the client, th[e] contractors who tender to build it, or by the consultants who design the wor[k] and ensure proper construction. But they will share a basic understanding o[f]

Fig. 117 (Below left) These men are drilling holes in the lining of a tunnel so that concrete can be pumped through to fill in the gaps behind it. (Balfour Beatty UK)

Fig. 118 (Below right) The operator of this drilling rig sits in an air-conditioned soundproofed cabin. (Atlas Copco Sweden)

Fig. 119 *These men are setting the explosive charges to blast the mountain rock. (Nitro Nobel AB Sweden)*

The name engineer was created in the 18th Century, from the French word 'genie', meaning ingenious. The hallmark of an engineer is indeed ingenuity, but he also needs to be creative and innovative, whether he is a Civil Engineer involved in the design and construction of power stations; a Mechanical Engineer designing and building machinery; an Electrical Engineer working on lighting systems and electronic components; or a Mining Engineer.

Fig. 120 *Operating the 'one hundred inch' hydraulic machine which was specially designed to be used on the 100" standard diameter tunnels through clay which provide water for London. (Edmund Nuttall UK)*

Fig. 121   *A tunneller on a drilling jumbo in a water tunnel. (Balfour Beatty UK)*

physics and mathematics and must be able to write reports, and have a degr in their engineering specialisation. The engineer in charge of a lar tunnelling project will have had many years postgraduate training while work, and will be qualified as a Chartered Civil Engineer.

Civil Engineers who work for consultants and contractors are employed over the world, often on single projects which last for years. Qualificatio gained in one country are generally accepted in others, though in pract companies tend to employ people trained in their own language. T international languages of tunnelling are mainly English, German a Japanese. Much of the manual and skilled artisan work of tunnelling is carri out by local people, and an engineer who has a working knowledge of the h country's language is more welcome and effective than one who hasn't.

Qualified engineers are often in demand. Currently in Britain there is acute shortage of experienced tunnel engineers needed to rebuild crumbli water and sewer tunnels. However, they are often not well paid in relation other professions, and since the days of the Favres, Brunels and their li lawyers and accountants have increased their control of client and contract organisations, to call the tune and reap the largest rewards. The engineeri profession is therefore anxious to encompass financial, entrepreneurial a management skills so as to ensure that engineers remain an influential bo

Women Engineers

Most engineers are men. The traditional prejudice which used to insist t women were unlucky on board ship was also common in mines and tunne Even today in some areas women are not expected, sometimes not allowed, enter tunnels under construction.

Engineering courses are open to women with mathematics and phys qualifications, though relatively few apply. Women who work on site tend have to prove themselves. As one said, 'It wasn't until I'd reached the top o 55m ladder five minutes ahead of the men that I ceased to be treated lik china doll.' Even when women who are well qualified join a group discussi in an office they can still have problems about being taken seriously i predominantly male environment. 'There were shocked faces when th realised I was going to talk about concrete rather than bring in the coff reported one training officer.

When the design of the tunnel has been decided and the go ahead given build, the equipment, materials and tunnellers have to be located and broug to the site. A detailed selection of methods of building the tunnel has to made; for instance, if a concrete lining is required, will it be provided in p fabricated sections or pumped and set inside the tunnel?

Other specialist engineers will decide on the content of the tunnel. Th include railway or highway engineers who specialise in transport tunne mechanical engineers who devise ventilation systems and pumps, wa engineers, safety specialists, electrical engineers who provide lighting a power supply and electronic control systems.

Use of Computers

Computer systems are used in deciding the alignment, lining, ventilati and lighting in tunnels, in estimating quantities of materials a programming work sequences. Computer personnel at all levels c therefore be involved in tunnelling.

Fig. 122 (Facing page) *Fitting temporary support during construction of a road tunnel using the New Austrian Tunnelling Method. (Beton und Monierbau Ges mbH Austria)*

Fig. 123 *Measuring the lighting in a Swiss road tunnel. (SGI Switzerland)*

Draughtsmen

Draughtsmen are employed in preparing plans for tunnel constructio often now using computers to help them.

Machine makers

Many people are involved in the manufacture and development machinery for tunnelling in which initiative and practical skills play a lar role once the basic mechanical, hydraulic, electronic designs and so on ha been prepared.

The people who physically build the tunnels are skilled miners, fitte carpenters and electricians who have learned the basics of their tra elsewhere and then specialised in tunnel work. Those operating expensi machinery need to be skilled, because carelessness can lead to death and del which can result in the contractor earning a bad reputation.

The Constant Noisy Bustle

Large bore tunnelling is a constant bustle of drillers operating jumb which create the blast holes for explosives, and for the rock bolts which ho back the face; of men operating tunnel boring machines, protected by shiel sometimes working in compressed air; of rockbolters and shotcreters; of st and concrete workers fitting the lining or grouting to seal out the water; truck loaders and conveyor operators getting rid of the spoil; of track a road layers, lighting and ventilation equipment fitters who finish off t tunnel.

A Test of Character

With all of this activity in a confined, often noisy underground spa tunnellers have to be hard working, committed teamworkers who can relied upon to do their part of the work properly and quickly.

A Sense of Achievement: The Creation of a Tunnel

Even those tunnellers who do not enjoy book learning and have ambition to be in charge need to understand the principles of constructi and machinery, and they share the satisfaction common to all those involv in civil engineering, of seeing something created by their own effort; a tunr that will serve people long beyond their own lifetimes.

Think of the satisfaction which could be yours if you become a tunnell and through a tunnel as important as the Channel Tunnel could say, 'I help to build this.'

Fig. 124 *This system was used to build a sewer tunnel in Hamburg Germany in 1984. The operator sits in his personal compre. air chamber and monitors the excavation. (T&T)*

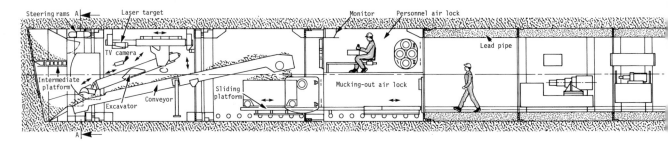

PHOTOFEATURE

Fig. 125   *A roadheader breaks through into a shaft to complete a sewer tunnel. (Mowlem UK)*

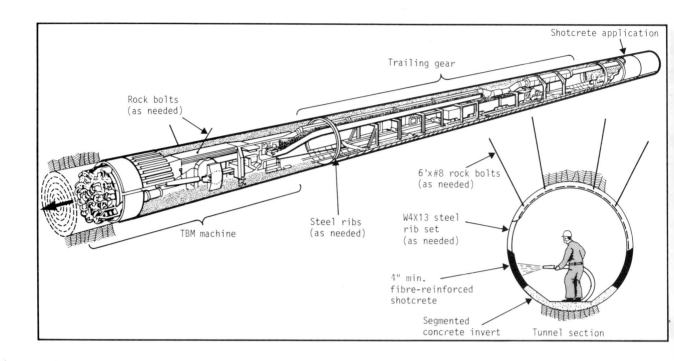

Fig. 126 *Diagram of boring machine used for drilling rock tunnels. (T&T)*

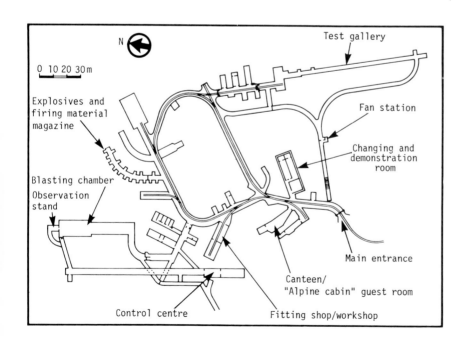

Fig. 127 *Equipment has to be tested before it can be used. This tunnel system in Switzerland has been especially built for such testing. (T&T)*

Fig. 128   *This Haggloader is clawing broken rock onto a conveyor. (Balfour Beatty UK)*

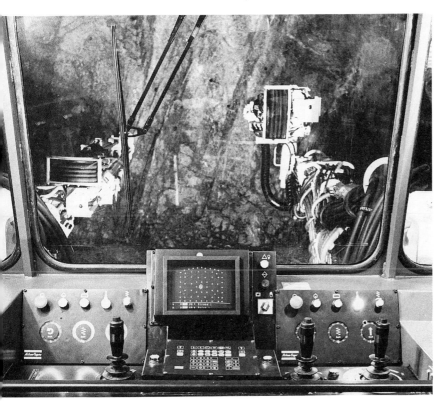

Fig. 129   *This robot rig can be programmed for a full cycle of work and left to get on with it. (Atlas Copco Sweden)*

Fig. 130 *This isn't a railway tunnel. It's the bottom of a sewer shaft. The railway system was installed just to carry materials while the sewer was under construction, then it was dismantled (Marti Inter Switzerland)*

Fig. 131   Precast concrete segments
such as these are used in many tunnels.
(Charcon Tunnels UK)

Fig. 132 *This telescopic shutter was placed in the tunnel and concrete flowed around it to create a lining. The process was continuous because the hydraulic 'horse' (Fig. 133 below) was used to bring sections of the shutter from the back when the concrete had set, to the front for new work. (Edmund Nuttall UK)*

Fig. 134 *When working in soft wet ground tunnellers are protected by shields as this tunneller building the Dartford road tunnel was. (Balfour Beatty UK)*

Fig. 135 *Another recent development in shield tunnelling is a system in which a suspension membrane holds back the ground while the operator remains in a control stand outside the compressed air area. (T&T)*

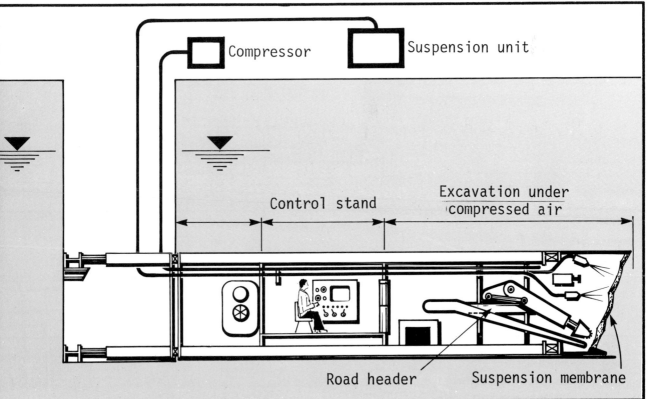

Compressor

Suspension unit

Control stand

Excavation under compressed air

Road header

Suspension membrane

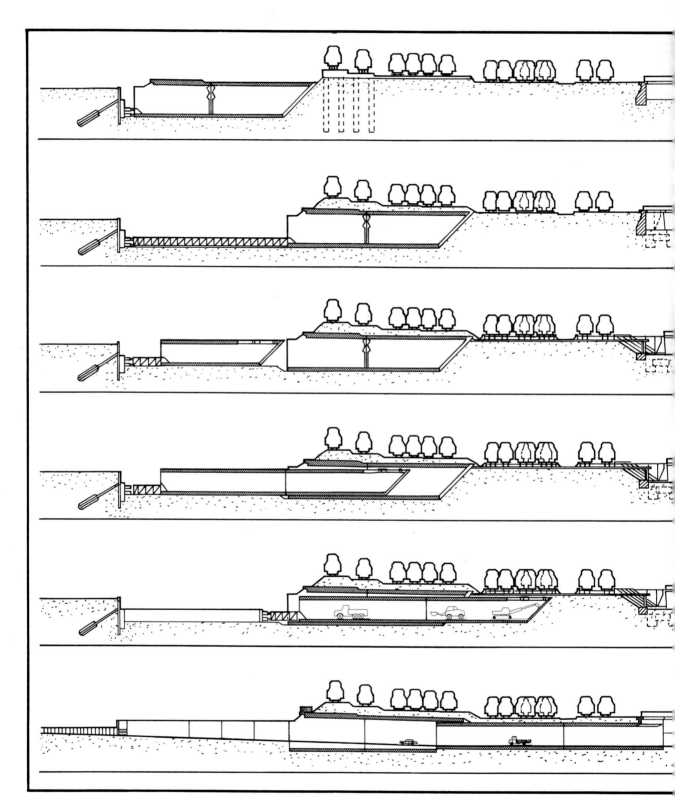

Fig. 136   *This sequence of diagrams shows how a tunnel is created when sections of a pipe are pushed through the ground us jacks. The technique is known as pipe-jacking. (T&T)*

Fig. 137 *A modern flexible hydraulically powered drilling rig. (Atlas Copco Sweden)*

Fig. 138 *Pipe jacking. Hydraulic jacks push a sewer pipe into place. (Buchan UK)*

Fig. 139 *Equipment which would seem massive if you stood next to it, can seem tiny when it is set to work in a giant cavern.* *for the bulldozer and dump truck in this photograph. (Edmund Nuttall UK)*
opposite page A rough hewn tailrace tunnel for used water after power generation for the Gitaru hydro-electric project in Kenya
(Balfour Beatty UK)

INDEX

A

Accountants 80
Africa 76
Air 12
Airport Tunnel 45
Alps 6, 26, 46, 49
Amsterdam 74
Ancient Mining 9–11
Appennine Tunnel, Gt 49
Aqueduct 21
Archaeologists 9
Arlberg Tunnel 53
Arctic Circle 25, 43
Ashford 74
Athens 11
Atlantic Ocean 76
Australia 17, 19
Austria 7, 9, 12, 16, 53

B

Barges 38
Bartlett, J. 55
Beaumont, Colonel 57,69
Belgium 12, 16, 35
Bentonite 55
Biosphere 36
Birmingham 22, 68
Blackwall Tunnel 55
Blasting 8, 47, 79
Blisworth 39
Bonaparte, Napoleon 67
Boulton, Matthew 17
Box Tunnel 40
Brandt, A. 49
Brazil 18
Bridgewater 38
Brindley Jones 38
Bristol 24
Britain 12
Brown, William 15
Brunel, Marc I. 54, 55
Brunel I.K. 40, 54, 68
Brussels 74

C

Cairo 24, 25
Calais 70, 71, 74
California 17, 25, 75
Cambodia 27
Canada 20, 21, 36, 45, 76
Canals 20, 21, 38
Car 43
Caverns 5, 35, 36, 76, 92
Caves 35, 36
CERN 28
Chadwick, E. 23
Chalk 72
Channel Tunnel 6, 67–74, 76
Chemicals 8
Cheriton 71
Chicago 3, 22, 24
China 3, 9, 16, 36
Choke damp 12
Cities 75, 76
Civil Engineer 78, 79, 80
Client 78
Coal 12, 14, 15, 18, 19, 38, 45, 57
Coal Cutter 15
Cochrane, Lord 15
Colombia 26
Colorado 17, 20
Compressed Air 48, 56, 57, 59, 82, 89
Computers 80
Construction 78
Consulting Engineers 78, 80
Contractors 80
Cooper Paul 76
Cornwall 12, 17
Corves 18, 19
Costing 78
Cyprus 9

D

Dartford Tunnel 43, 55
Denmark 76
Denver 50
Derbyshire 12

D (cont.)

Design 78
Devon 12
Diamonds 17–19
Diamond Drills 46, 67
Dinorwig 30, 31
Dover 68, 69
Drainage 9, 23–24
Draughtsmen 82
Drilling 20, 29, 78, 91
Drills 15–16, 46, 52–66
Dynamite 8

E

Earth 6
Edinburgh 25
Egypt 24
Egyptians 9
Eisenhower Tunnel 53
Elbe Tunnel 59
Electrical Engineers 80
Energy 35
Engineers 78
Eurotunnel 72–73
Excavation 7, 72
Explosives 16, 47–48, 79

F

Favre, L. 47
Finland 24
Fire 9, 45
Firedamp 13
Fitters 82
Fjords 76
Folkestone 68, 71
Fox, C.J. 67
France 12, 16, 74
Freight 45
Funckel, Johannes 14
Future 75

ammond Aimé 67
ases 8, 35
atwick Airport 45
elatine 47
eologist 78
ermany 12, 16, 35, 45
ibralter 76
old 11, 17
ravity 6
reathead Shield 55
reeks 11
unpowder 9, 15

ard Rock 8, 9, 15
arecastle 38
eat 8
elsinki 24
ighway Engineers 80
ong Kong 24, 40, 59
oosac Tunnel 48
orses 17, 19
udson River 57
umbolt 13
ungary 14
ydro-electricity 25, 26, 29–32

mersed Tube 56, 76
dia 18, 75
donesia 32
rigation 22–23
rael 9
tanbul 24
aly 12
an the Terrible 21

pan 26, 49, 58, 59, 76
rsey 44
rusalem 11
mbos 21, 29, 80

aymakli 35
ent 74
enya 26, 27
ilsby Tunnel 39
onkola Mine 17

L

Lamps 13, 14
Laser 8
Lawyers 80
Lead 11
Leeds 23
Lewis 49
Leyner 16
Light 13, 14
Liverpool 22, 39
Living underground 35
Locke, J. 68
Locomotive 18
Loetschberg Tunnel 49
London 40, 41, 74
Low, William 69

M

Machinery 82
Macmillan, Harold 70
Manchester 22
Marshall, James W. 17
Mathematics 78, 80
Mathieu, A. 67
Mechanical Engineers 79, 80
Mechanics 78
Medieval 12, 13
Mersey River 57, 60–66, 69, 77
Metro Tunnels 40
Middle Ages 12–13
Milan 47
Mines 10–11, 12–17, 35
Mining 13–20
Mining Engineers 78–79
Moffat Tunnel 49
Mont Blanc Tunnel 50
Mont Cenis Tunnel 46
Mountain 46–50, 53

N

Navvies 39
Naples 11
Napoleon 68
New Austrian Tunnelling
  Method 53, 80
New York 22, 24, 55, 57, 59
New Zealand 49
Newcomen, Thomas 17
Newton, I. 6
Nitroglycerine 47, 48
Nobel, Alfred 16, 47
Norway 25, 36, 43, 47, 76
Nuclear Waste 36

O

Oil 35
Ophir Mine 12
Ore 14–17, 19

P

Pacific Ocean 76
Pakistan 22
Panama Canal 76
Paris 22, 47, 67, 70, 74
Physics 78
Pipe Jacking 90, 91
Planners 78
Poland 12
Portal 5, 51
Potash 35
Power Supply 4, 24, 29–32, 75
Pressure 6
Primrose Hill Tunnel 39

Q

Queen Elizabeth 66

R

Railway 39, 40, 45, 48, 49
Railway Engineers 80
Ramsey, D. 17
Red Sea 22
Rheims 74
Rhodes, Cecil 18
Roadheader 15, 44, 83
Roads 11, 21, 50, 51, 52, 53
Robbins 3
Robots 76
Rock Bolts 12
Rockies 6, 45, 49, 50, 53
Romans 11, 21
Russia 16, 17, 27, 36

S

Safety 73
Saigon 27
Saint Barbara 12
Samos 11
San Francisco 22
Sangatte 71, 72
Saudi Arabia 22
Saxony 12
Sciences 28, 78
Scotland 25

Seam 15
Seattle 25
Segments, Tunnel 70, 87
Seikan 58
Selby 16
Severn, Tunnel 56
Sewers 21, 23–24, 82, 83
Sewerage 22, 23–24, 26
Shaft 5, 19, 39, 54
Shape 5, 7
Shields 55, 89
Shotcrete 5
Shutter 88
Silver 11, 17
Simplon Tunnel 49
Singapore 38
Skills 82
Smeaton, John 17
Soft Ground 8, 15
Sommeiller 46–47
South Africa 13, 18, 19, 23, 26, 45
South America 14, 17
Spain 12, 23
Sports 36
Sri Lanka 7, 23, 29
St. Bernard 50
St. Gotthard 46
Steam 16, 18, 19
Stephenson, G. 18, 39, 68
Storage 35, 36
Stress 6
Surveyors 78
Swaziland 9

Sweden 12, 16, 25, 35, 36, 75, 76
Switzerland 28, 34
Sydney 59

T

Tanna Tunnel 49
Technology 8, 76
Terrenoir Tunnel 39
Thames, River 54
Thatcher, Margaret 70
Tokyo 26, 59
Totley Tunnel 40
Transport 38–45
Trevithick, R. 17, 18, 54
Tungsten 17
Tunnel Boring Machine 4, 67, 68, 69, 70, 72
Tunnellers 82
Tunnelling Today 77
Tunnelling Tomorrow 77
Turin 47
Turkey 35
Tyne Tunnel 56

U

Underwater 54–66
Uranium 20
USA 12, 15, 16, 17, 20, 21, 24, 26, 28, 36, 40, 48, 49, 75

V

Vanadium 17
Varda 43
Ventilation 12, 13, 38, 39, 50, 57, 68, 69
Victoria, Queen 68
Vietnam 27

W

Walker, T. 56
Wapping Tunnel 39
War 27
Waste 35, 36
Water 7, 16, 17, 47, 54, 79
Water Supply 11, 22
Watkin, Sir Edward 69–70
Watt, James 17
Whitaker 68
Wigan 15
Wolseley, Sir Garnet 69
Women 80
Woolf 17

Z

Zambia 17
Zimbabwe 12
Zurich 47